WANG WEI & SF EXPRESS

A BUSINESS AND LIFE BIOGRAPHY

Published by
LID Publishing
An imprint of LID Business Media Ltd.
The Record Hall, Studio 304,
16-16a Baldwins Gardens,
London EC1N 7RJ, UK

info@lidpublishing.com
www.lidpublishing.com

A member of:
BPR
businesspublishersroundtable.com

Published in collaboration with the China Translation & Publishing House
(a member of the China Publishing Group Corporation)
Proofread by Li Hui and Liu Dan.

CTPH China Translation and Publishing House

Printed in the United States
ISBN: 978-1-912555-47-5
ISBN: 978-1-911671-78-7 (ebook)

Illustration: Benson Koo
Cover and page design: Caroline Li

WANG WEI & SF EXPRESS

A BUSINESS AND LIFE BIOGRAPHY

BY **ZHOU XIBING**

TRANSLATED BY **CHANG YUAN** AND **LI JIAJING**

LID

MADRID | MEXICO CITY | LONDON
NEW YORK | BUENOS AIRES
BOGOTA | SHANGHAI | NEW DELHI

CONTENTS

Guided by the spirit of craftsmanship, SF Express is committed to conducting multi-angled research on Chinese enterprises by engaging in the stories behind each brand. We aim to carry forward the craftsmanship DNA of each brand to help create long-lasting names.

Our business partners include Alibaba, Apple, Carpenter Tan, Giant, Gome, Gree Electric, Huawei, Laoganma, Lenovo, Toyota, Tsingtao Brewery, Wahaha, XCMG Group and Yunguan Orange (Chu's Orange).

FIVE STAGES OF SF EXPRESS'S DEVELOPMENT

TODAY

2012–TODAY
Strategic Transformation
Optimize the assignment of responsibilities, carry out customer-centred operation transformation, provide integrated supply chain solution services, consolidate leading position in the field of B2B express industry, and initiate a big move into the e-commerce field with higher goals.

2008–2012
Leading the Competition
Build its own airlines, go global gradually and strengthen competitive advantages.

2002–2007
Management Optimization
Set up headquarters, comprehensively improve management, standardize business network and provide better services for customers.

1997–2001
High-Speed Growth
Go out of South China and go national with rapid growth.

1993–1997
Start-up
Difficult business start-up in the Pearl River Delta area.

CHAPTER 1

THE ORIGINS OF SF EXPRESS

When we talk about catching up with international champion express enterprises, in what aspects should we catch up with them? First of all, I think, it is not a matter of scale, but the quality of their service, their popularity, and their pursuit of consumers' recognition and social respect that matter. Secondly, it is necessary to evaluate our own capacity to realize such a goal. Construction on a shaky foundation is most likely to end up with an unstable building, or even with disaster. We need to make a clear assessment of ourselves and to advance with a steady pace. As for how fast we can go, or how far we can forward our steps, there's no necessity to make any excessive demands. Thirdly, most of our efforts depend on the sustaining stability of our national industrial policy.

– Wang Wei

HARD WORK IS THE ONLY GUARANTEE OF SUCCESS

Throughout China's thousands of years of history, each era has witnessed the emergence of numerous talents in all fields. These people have contributed to the greatness and splendour of Chinese civilization.

"In each generation there would emerge outstanding people, who respectively led the trend for several hundred years." These lines, written by Zhao Yi, a poet of the Qing dynasty (1644–1912), are a brief sketch of how Chinese talents have pushed forward the development of history like waves of the Yangtze River, and how they have composed heroic songs of their own time. That is also the case for the period of reform and opening-up in China.

Since the initiation of policies relating to reform and opening-up, China's economy has undergone vigorous growth. During this time, many entrepreneurs have managed to lead their companies into the ranks of the world's top 500 businesses. One of them is Wang Wei, who founded SF Express, the Chinese version of FedEx. Wang not only created his own express enterprise but has also excelled among various giant rivals at home and abroad, thus becoming a veritable 'potential champion.'

After the back-door listing of SF on 23 February 2017, this newly visible public company finally revealed itself to the attentive media and society. Thanks to a series of reports, we are now able to learn about its unknown history and Wang, and to begin an insightful journey into the full scope of the company's development.

Through its back-door listing, SF Express successfully went public with a market value reaching over ¥100 billion. At the height of this manoeuvre, Wang's personal wealth soared to third place in the Chinese mainland, surpassing Ma Huateng, the founder of Tencent, and ranking only behind Wang Jianlin, the founder of Wanda, and Jack Ma, the founder of Alibaba.

As a child, Wang Wei moved from the mainland to Hong Kong. As an adult, he experienced an astounding rise from a petty businessman at the bottom of society to a tycoon with hundreds of billions in wealth. The same is true of SF Express, which has evolved from a little-known start-up company on a street in the Shunde District, Foshan, Guangdong Province, to a leading express delivery giant in China. What kind of magic strategy did Wang employ to enable him to pave such an impressive path for his start-up? In truth, it has been a path of hardships and frustrations, yet it is legendary and, as such, arouses our curiosity.

So, let us turn the clock back to 1978, a turning point for both China and the founder of SF Express, a seven-year-old at the time. Looking back at 1978, we can fully appreciate the sharp turn this boy was to experience: from the superior life of a Shanghai middle-class family to a stressful life in Hong Kong.

A YEAR OF TRANSMUTATION

On 11 May 1978, *Guangming Daily* published an article on its front page titled "Practice is the Sole Criterion of Truth." It pointed out that the criterion of truth can only be realized through social practice, and the integration of theory and practice is the most basic Marxist principle. The publication of this article was hailed as "spring thunder" by rational theorists in China, triggering a heated discussion on "what should be the standard of truth."

From 18 to 22 December that year, the third plenary session of the 11th Central Committee of the Communist Party of China was held in Beijing. The main task of the session was to shift the focus of the whole Party to socialist modernization.

The plenary session made the strategic decision to shift the focus of the Party's work to socialist modernization from 1979. On the issue of economic construction, in order to rectify the erroneous tendency of rushing for results and to solve the serious imbalance between the main portions of the national economy, the Party needed to take a series of new and important measures and start a serious reform of the over-centralized economic management system.

The plenary session redefined the correct ideological line of the Communist Party of China, criticized the wrong policy of the "Two Whatevers,"[1] fully affirmed the need to master and apply the scientific system of Mao Zedong's thought in a complete and accurate way, strongly approved discussions on the standard of truth, and determined the guiding principles of "emancipating the mind, setting wits to work, seeking truth from facts and looking forward in unity."[2]

This conclusion fundamentally negated the principle of the "Two Whatevers." Subsequently, China's process of reform and opening-up was initiated.

A thousand kilometres away, the situation was in stark contrast to the drastic social changes taking place in Beijing: a couple in Shanghai were as yet unaware of the coming era of change in China. After much deliberation, they made the decision to move to Hong Kong.

The couple were none other than the parents of Wang Wei, who was then only seven years old, too young to participate in his parents' discussion. Thus, in 1978, Wang and his family moved to Hong Kong for a new life. Back then, none of them realized this move would change the course of the seven-year-old's life forever.

Like other people driven by what is known as the 'tide of going to Hong Kong,' after settling there, Wang and his family had to deal with an environment totally different from that of the mainland. The truth is, the newly arrived mainland residents not only accelerated the prosperity of Hong Kong but also created innumerable stories of entrepreneurship, such as those about the 'Lion Rock Spirit' – touching stories that record the struggles of people at the lower levels of Hong Kong society (see more below).

From the 1940s to the 1980s, there were several waves of migration from the mainland to Hong Kong. Such a large number of migrants brought in the labour force, skills, capital and (most importantly) highly-qualified talent that Hong Kong urgently needed during that time and even today.

This explains why, with the ebb and flow of the historical tide, Hong Kong, which is situated far from the political centre of Beijing, experienced its economic take-off at this time. Each day, when night fell and the flashing neon lights came on, the flourishing night scene in Hong Kong was vividly delineated.

Many people cannot help recalling the charming and luxurious golden age of Shanghai in the era of the Republic of China (1912–1949). Nevertheless, for historical reasons, talent and capital from the mainland was successively flying south to Hong Kong, which contributed to its prosperity.

At the time, it was common to see scenes featuring glamorous neon lights in Hong Kong movies. In the eyes of Hong Kong directors at the time, neon lights were not only a visual symbol but also integrated the prosperity of Hong Kong with the inspiring and touching stories of the whole nation. Later on, as the stories of Hong Kong heroes spread all over the world, the influence of Hong Kong movies was fully manifested. For example, in the Korean TV series *Reply 1988*, a clip of the Hong Kong film *A Better Tomorrow* (1986) was included at the very beginning of each episode.

Meanwhile, with its reputation as the 'Oriental Pearl' of the world, Hong Kong gradually became recognized as part of the 'newly industrial economies' or 'Four Dragons of Asia,' together with Korea, Singapore and Taiwan.

In such a context, the neon lights – the barometer of Hong Kong's economy – indicated the ushering in of a new golden age. At that time, Hong Kong people, who liked to hum the theme song from the TV series *Below the Lion Rock*, truly believed that hard work would yield success, no matter whether the situation was favourable or adverse.

THE LION ROCK SPIRIT

The Lion Rock in Hong Kong is only 495 metres above sea level. It is not high enough to be introduced in detail in any of Hong Kong's guidebooks. However, there are many folklore tales about the origins of the Lion Rock. One version is that in ancient times there were nine dragons, who often wreaked havoc on people. To protect these wretched folk, the Jade Emperor dispatched a lion to suppress the dragons, and this created the landscape.

There are many other narratives related to the place, especially ones that tell of legendary achievements under the Lion Rock during the economic take-off of Hong Kong. There are examples of entrepreneurship occurring by the side of Lion Rock itself, and the TV series *Below the Lion Rock* became popular in mainland China. As a result of these and other phenomena, 'Lion Rock spirit' is regarded as a synonym for the hard work and arduous striving of Hong Kong's people.

In the 1940s and 1950s, the Kuomintang and the Chinese Communist Party were still fighting each other. At this time, Liu Jinmu, a native of Chaoyang in Guangdong Province in his early twenties, left his hometown, crossed the Shenzhen River and the Kowloon Peninsula, and moved forward into Hong Kong. Undeniably, it was Liu's past experiences that had prompted him to venture into this new world: he had lost his father when he was aged seven and his mother when he was aged nine. The purpose of his flight to Hong Kong with a group of villagers was to escape the war and to save his life.

When Liu and the villagers arrived at the Lion Rock, they found that their predecessors had erected many disordered wooden houses at the foot of the hill, whose peak looks like a mighty lion. Like the other villagers, Liu had to cut down trees from the hillside to build a wooden house of his own. After he gained a stable foothold, he found himself a job as a dock worker in Sai Wan. Through his own efforts, Liu, the young man from Chaoyang, became totally integrated into Hong Kong society.

More than 20 years later, in the 1970s, when a song named "Below the Lion Rock" became popular, Liu's fourth son often hummed it. To him, its lyrics depicted the stories of struggle and happiness of his own family.[3]

In 2002, when Hong Kong was facing an economic downturn, the then financial secretary, Antony Leung Kam-chung, after announcing his first budget statement, recited the lyrics of "At the Foot of the Lion Rock" to encourage Hong Kong's people to acquire and develop the Lion Rock spirit. On 19 November 2002, Zhu Rongji, the then premier of the People's Republic of China, also mentioned the lyrics and called on Hong Kong's people to start their businesses anew.

This song describes not only the entrepreneurial efforts and struggles at the poorer levels of society but also their tenacity and undefeatable spirit in the 1970s, when Hong Kong started to prosper. It also vividly portrays the image of the 'new Hong Kong people' who left the mainland for Hong Kong in waves of immigration, unceasingly striving to create better lives, like Wang Wei. The Lion Rock spirit has become the symbol of hard work and striving for a better life in Hong Kong. Lin Zhenhua, an entrepreneur, said: "When the economy was at its lowest, we would often talk about it [the Lion Rock spirit] to encourage each other. We believed that as long as we faced the obstacles bravely, tomorrow would be better."

So, on the one hand, Wang Wei's success today stems from his own efforts and perseverance and on the other hand, it is inseparable from the Lion Rock spirit.

A CHANGED ENTREPRENEURIAL LIFE

When we look back at the history of Hong Kong from the 1940s to the 1980s, a period featuring this large wave of migration to Hong Kong, it is clear that the fates of thousands of people changed, including that of the seven-year-old Wang Wei.

In 1971, Wang Wei was born into a well-off intellectual family in Shanghai. His father was a Russian–Chinese interpreter for the air force and his mother was a teacher at a university in Jiangxi Province. Even today, their professions are very respectable, let alone in the 1970s.

As is widely known, since Shanghai opened its port in 1842, it has transformed from a small fishing village to one of the largest cities in the Far East in terms of finance and trade. Wang Tao, a renowned reformist thinker in the late Qing dynasty, described in detail the tremendous changes that occurred after Shanghai's opening as a commercial port in his book *The Miscellaneous Records of Yingruan*:

> *As the maritime trade ban was lifted, graves abandoned for thousands of years were transformed into splendid mansions. Alas! When people indulged*

themselves in wine, the wisp was shivering in the daylilies. Pressed on the riverside were pavilions reaching to the clouds in the sky, stretching upward to the dimly discernible palaces of immortals. A world of exotics unfolded, as if I was on a journey to Western countries.

From that point, over more than a hundred years, Shanghai developed to become one of the financial centres of mainland China. Even during the Second Sino-Japanese War (1937–1945), it still played an important role in regional finance.

After the founding of the People's Republic of China in 1949, Shanghai maintained its financial status. In the late 1970s, it remained the most developed city in China. According to GDP data, Shanghai ranked first among the nine major cities of China in 1978, with more than twice as much as Beijing, the capital of China. The details are as follows: (1) Shanghai's GDP was ¥27.28 billion, (2) Beijing's GDP was ¥10.88 billion, (3) Tianjin's GDP was ¥8.27 billion, (4) Chongqing's GDP was ¥6.73 billion, (5) Changchun's GDP was ¥5.12 billion, (6) Harbin's GDP was ¥4.57 billion, (7) Shenyang's GDP was ¥4.40 billion, (8) Guangzhou's GDP was ¥4.31 billion and (9) Wuhan's GDP was ¥3.91 billion. In 2018, Shanghai's GDP reached over ¥3.2 trillion, an increase of 6.6% over 2017 and 120 times that of 1978.

Nevertheless, in 1978, Wang Wei's parents decided to move to Hong Kong from Shanghai. Unfortunately, what they didn't anticipate was that their migration would not bring a better life but an extremely poor one instead. This was because Hong Kong, a British colony at that time, recognized neither academic nor working qualifications gained in the Chinese mainland. Consequently, Wang's parents could only engage in relatively low-end jobs. Their living conditions plummeted; the family income declined to an extent that it was a significant challenge simply to make a living, a situation in sharp contrast with their previously comfortable life in Shanghai.

Even worse, Wang had to quit school. According to traditional Chinese culture, children born into intellectual families are supposed to be devoted to their studies. They are expected to study at famous universities at home or abroad. After graduation, they are expected to return home, get a better job than their parents' and maintain the family honour. But Wang, in the hope of easing his parents' burden, gave up the chance to go to university after leaving high school. He found a position as an unskilled labourer in his uncle's factory.

Hong Kong in the 1970s and 1980s witnessed many people like Wang who would do odd jobs rather than continue into higher education. For them, going to university meant high tuition fees and an uncertain future, so people commonly preferred to get a job and gradually accumulate money. Making money first and getting a diploma second was the natural choice.

In 1972, Hong Kong TV aired the aforementioned show named *Below the Lion Rock*, which showed stories of ordinary people starting a business through self-improvement, diligence and seeking prosperity in adversity. Years later, Wang recalled in an interview that:

When my family moved to Hong Kong, we were faced with extreme poverty. We had to start everything

> *from scratch. My parents used to be university professors in the mainland, but their diplomas were not recognized in Hong Kong, so they had to work as manual workers to earn low wages. I've experienced the poor life; I know quite well what it's like to be penniless and discriminated against.*

These words indicate the tremendous change of situation experienced by the family, and how a boy with a sense of superiority back home was reminded of the gap between the mainland and Hong Kong. Without the security of his parents' previous high-level educational background and stable family finances, he had to start everything from scratch.

Like many other underprivileged people, Wang stopped studying after graduating from high school and gave up the dream of becoming a member of the elite through education. Instead, he began to explore another way to live. Working as a labourer for his uncle, he moved through the hustle and bustle of the gilded city of Hong Kong, looking forward to his own golden opportunities.

Wang's ambition was gradually stirred. In contrast to many others at the time, he was quite certain that only people who knew how to take advantage of the situation could seize the opportunity, and only those who worked hard would win.

STARTING POINT: SHUNDE

If you want to succeed, you must seize the opportunity while working hard and dare to take risks while struggling, otherwise you will never make it. Such thoughts, like sparks that ignite the whole prairie, were pounding within Wang Wei's restless and striving heart.

Just like Mark Li, the hero in the film *A Better Tomorrow*, said, "I don't want to be trampled on all through my life! You think I'm a bum? I have had bad luck for three years, just waiting for a chance! I'll fight for my dignity, not to prove that I am greater than others, but to tell people, I will take back whatever I lost!"

Whereas many other migrants complained all day, Wang chose to start his own business in Shunde District, Foshan, Guangdong Province. He was aware of the vast opportunities in the emerging mainland market, following the intensified process of reform and opening-up.

In 1992, Deng Xiaoping, the chief architect of China's reform and opening-up, visited Shenzhen, which started a new surge of investment. Later, Deng Xiaoping delivered a series of speeches during his inspection tour of South China. In these speeches, Deng said:

> *In such a short period of less than two decades, our country has developed so fast, which has delighted the people and attracted the attention of the world. It has incontrovertibly proved the correctness of the principles and policies that we have been holding since the third plenary session of the 11th Communist Party of China (CPC) Central Committee. Undeniably, we will stick to such principles and policies. Since the reform and opening-up, we have set quite a few specific rules and regulations in various fields including the economy, politics, science and technology, education, culture, the military and foreign affairs. The eighth plenary session of the 13th CPC Central*

Committee was a successful meeting. The reason why we think highly of this meeting is that it decided the rural household contract responsibility system, which will be implemented continuously, which assured our people that the general policies of the Central Committee would remain unchanged.

In the early period of rural reform, there was a brand of roasted melon seeds from Anhui named 'Shaziguazi' (Fool's Melon Seeds).[4] Its founder, who used to be a nobody, became a millionaire at that time, which made many people feel uncomfortable, saying that he would be punished. However, I refused to act in that way. If we did this, people would think that the policy had changed, which would do more harm than good. There are still quite a few problems of this kind. If not handled properly, they are likely to undermine our guidelines and thus affect the overall reform. The basic policies for urban and rural reform must remain stable in the long run. Of course, in the course of implementation, the policies will be improved and adjusted, but the general direction should be unswerving. We will not risk our reform for new ideas. As long as we hold this belief, there is great hope for China.

In Deng's view, only by continuing reform and opening-up could China maintain its prosperity and stability. After Deng's Southern Inspection Tour, China thus ushered in a new boom of entrepreneurship. On this tide, Wang Wei, with his insight into business opportunities, began his business life in Shunde.

OPPORTUNITY FAVOURS ONLY THE PREPARED MIND

Once, when giving a lecture to some CEOs about the management concept of Laoganma,[5] I mentioned Wang Wei. At the time, one entrepreneur complained about the current business environment, particularly the unilateralism of 'de-globalization' in the United States. To back up his point, he took the US government blocking Huawei as an example.

I once wrote an article titled "The Lighthouse is Waiting for an Early Return of the Dusk Boat," discussing whether Huawei would change its direction in going global. The article attracted the attention of many foreign media outlets, including *The Wall Street Journal*, *Forbes* and *The Globe and Mail*. Both in this article and in the following interviews, I mentioned that when facing the pressure imposed by the United States, Huawei should by no means change its existing route in going out into the world, and should only make minor adjustments.

So, in response to the aforementioned entrepreneur's complaint, I gave examples of entrepreneurs since the reform and opening-up (such as Tao Huabi, the founder of Laoganma; Ren Zhengfei, the founder of Huawei; Zong Qinghou, the founder of Wahaha; Tan Chuanhua, the founder of Carpenter Tan; and Wang Wei, the founder of SF Express) whose stories show that bad market environments are common in doing business, especially for those businesses that have survived for hundreds of years. Just as the English writer Charles Dickens wrote in *A Tale of Two Cities*:

> *It was the best of times, it was the worst of times, it was the age of wisdom, it was the age of foolishness, it was the epoch of belief, it was the epoch of incredulity, it was the season of Light, it was the season of Darkness, it was the spring of hope, it was the winter of despair;*

> *we had everything before us, we had nothing before us, we were all going direct to Heaven, we were all going direct the other way.*

When opportunities come, only those who dare to dream and to adventure can take their first step in starting businesses. Then what they need to do is provide customers with the best products and services.

Wang Wei set a good example. Back in the 1990s, after Deng's Southern Inspection Tour speech, he took the risk of going north to Shunde, where he established a printing and dyeing enterprise, and later found business opportunities in delivery goods.

Undeniably, thousands of entrepreneurs were aware of such a business opportunity, but why was it only Wang who seized it? The reason is that in any era, an opportunity – or even a stroke of luck – favours only the prepared mind.

In the 1990s, Hong Kong's factories began to move to the north with their capital and technology, and mostly clustered in the Pearl River Delta region in Guangdong Province. The mode of economic cooperation between Hong Kong and the Pearl River Delta region is vividly called 'shop in the front, factory in the back.' This mode, together with the unique geographical relationship between Hong Kong and Guangdong, has facilitated businesses based on mail, goods and other exchanges between the two places. A group of 'itinerant traders' sprang up, and Wang was one of them.

However, in contrast to the others, Wang saw the potential commercial value in the situation and concluded that an express business would become a new way to make a fortune. On this topic, Li Hongxia, a reporter for *Business China*, once wrote:

> *The size of a tree is not measured by its branches, but by its roots. Different people have different opinions when it comes to the seizing of opportunities. Playing the market only brings temporary glory, but in fact both one's career and one's life are like a marathon. The real competition relies on strength. Of course, even when the opportunity is a godsend, it is only so for those who are well prepared.*

To Li, "One must be strong enough to forge iron." Wang's success needed to be built on the basis of his company's strength, and this strength needed to encompass not only the modern facilities and magnificent financial data that people could easily see but also a suitable management system and corporate culture that would unite employees together.[6]

WANG WEI THE 'ITINERANT TRADER'

Wang Wei chose Shunde to start his printing and dyeing business because it was adjacent to prosperous cities such as Guangzhou, Jiangmen and Zhongshan. Moreover, Shunde was a pioneer at the time of reform and opening-up. In the 1980s, the first experimental form of 'three-plus-one' trading (i.e. custom manufacturing with materials, designs or samples supplied and compensation trade) in China took shape in Shunde. This indicated the government's strong support for the development of township enterprises, thus making Shunde one of the 'Four Tigers of Guangdong.'[7]

According to the government website of Shunde District in Foshan, Shunde is a major region for the private economy with manufacturing as its pillar industry. Private industries consist of 77% of the gross output value of above-average-scale companies in the whole region. Shunde is one of the largest manufacturing bases for air conditioners, refrigerators, water heaters and sterilizers in China. It is also the largest supply base for rice cookers and microwave ovens in the world, and has earned 28 national honorary titles, such as "Capital of Chinese Electrical Appliances," "Capital of Gas Stoves of China" and "Hometown of Chinese Coating Materials." After years of development, Shunde has fostered various concentrated types of industrial group, with an output value exceeding ¥200 billion: two world top-500 enterprises (Midea Group and Country Garden Holdings Company Ltd), 39 mainstay private enterprises with investment exceeding ¥1 billion, and a number of 'potential champion' enterprises that are influential both at home and abroad.[8]

Additionally, Shunde has been rich in natural resources and has been economically well-developed since ancient times. Hundreds of years ago, in the Ming and Qing dynasties, Shunde was known as the "Developed County of Lingnan," the "Southern Silk Capital" and the "Bank of Guangdong" for its thriving dike-pond farming, silk-reeling industry, and financial and trade industries.[9]

As is widely known, a place of prosperity often breeds outstanding talent. The local celebrities of Shunde's history are as follows: three first-rank advanced scholars (*zhuangyuan*, a title conferred on the champion at the highest level of imperial examination), one first-rank advanced martial talent (*wu zhuangyuan*, a title conferred on the champion at the highest level of imperial martial arts examination), 762 advanced scholars and martial talents (*wen jinshi* and *wu jinshi*, candidates at the highest level of examination in the capital) and 2,397 recommended men (*wen juren* and *wu juren*, candidates at the provincial level of examination). Other figures include Li Jian, an intellectual in the Qing dynasty who was good at poetry, calligraphy and painting; Su Renshan, an eccentric painter; and many other remarkable people, such as Bruce Lee, Lee Shau-kee, Cheng Yu-tung, Law Ting-pong, Wu Yee-sun, Leung Kau-kui and Margaret Chan.[10]

Because of the convenient transportation, developed commerce and pool of talent in Shunde, Wang Wei resolutely chose this place to start his business. Initially, like most entrepreneurs, he did not make much profit. But his small printing and dyeing project allowed him to notice a huge opportunity, which would radically change the path of his entrepreneurship.

When running his printing and dyeing business, Wang found that in the process of production, manufacturers needed to send product samples to their customers for confirmation. Mass production would not start until the customers had tested the samples and confirmed their approval. Wang's factory also needed to follow this process. However, each sample, even the urgent ones, could take an unbearably long time to be forwarded. This sample inspection process greatly affected the scheduling and completion of orders, as well as the efficiency and cost of production.

As is widely said, "Where there are complaints, there are business opportunities." While some company owners were complaining about the prolonged inspection cycle, others saw potential business opportunities. The latter started a new business to help Hong Kong's entrepreneurs who had set up factories in Guangdong to carry their sample goods from Guangdong to Hong Kong.

Wang, who was troubled by the time-consuming inspection cycle and often had to send his samples to Hong Kong via the new method, soon recognized that it was a good way to improve efficiency. Business owners called these people who collected and transported their goods 'itinerant traders,' as they shuttled between Shenzhen (on the mainland) and Hong Kong every day, carrying goods with them.

As a Hong Kong investor on the mainland, Wang naturally started to make deals with these itinerant traders. Sometimes Wang himself acted as an itinerant trader to help his business partners to carry goods to Hong Kong. In the initial stages, when working as an itinerant trader, Wang didn't charge any fees. Sometimes his partners who entrusted goods to him would feel sorry for troubling him, and they would try to give him a reasonable reward, but Wang never accepted them.

THE BIRTH OF SF EXPRESS

The volume of goods entrusted to Wang became larger and larger. Once there were so many items that Wang Wei's luggage was not large enough to hold them. By then, Wang had become aware of the blue waters of a huge market.

In the early 1990s, when Hong Kong entrepreneurs saw the potential market and productive capacities after China's reform and opening-up, more than 80,000 manufacturing enterprises moved from Hong Kong to the mainland. Of these, more than 50,000 were located in the Pearl River Delta.

This led to a surge of mail and cargo traffic between Hong Kong and the Pearl River Delta. At that time, due to certain policies and a restrictive economic environment, there were many unsolved problems, such as tariff barriers between Hong Kong and the mainland, which made freight and logistics a headache for these business owners.

Inspired by his previous experiences, Wang began a strategic business transformation, aiming to solve this problem. After some careful consideration, he resolutely left the still lucrative printing and dyeing industry and decided to move into the field of professional express delivery.

After returning to Hong Kong, Wang told his father about his ideas. His father agreed with him on the necessity of founding a professional delivery service company, and provided HK$100,000 for Wang to start his new business.

With his father's support, especially with the HK$100,000 as a start-up fund, Wang immediately returned to Shunde and completed all the required procedures to set up Shunfeng, his delivery service company. Then he rushed back to Hong Kong and rented a shop of less than 20 square metres on Portland Street between Mongkok and Prince Edward Road. At the time, the main business of this small company was to deliver letters from Hong Kong enterprises to the Pearl River Delta. In this way, driven by market demand, SF Express was born.

FOUNDER, CAPTAIN, COURIER

In the 1990s, the company consisted of only six men, including Wang. As the founder of a company in its early stages of development, Wang had to handle everything just like other start-up entrepreneurs. In order to speed up deliveries and improve services for their clients, Wang and his five employees collected and delivered parcels almost around the clock. In these years, whether it was windy or rainy, Wang and his employees would busily travel around Shunde, leaving their footprints at every corner of the city. Even if they accidentally fell down, they would manage to get up and continue their delivery.

Nowadays, Wang seldom collects or delivers, but sometimes he does like to go through the delivering procedure again by himself, to commemorate the various scars left on his legs by his previous work.

Years later, a fellow worker who experienced the earlier rough times with Wang, recalled that: "At that time, we ate and lived together. The only daily task was to take orders. It seemed that we were almost frenzied! Day and night we were on motorbikes, shuttling across streets and alleys to deliver goods."

It was through this experience that Wang came to understand the living conditions of every single courier. And it is because of this knowledge that he is always ready to fight for couriers' rights.

In the afternoon of 17 April 2016, a video titled "A Young SF Delivery Guy was Slapped in the Face" spread across all major Chinese social media sites on the internet. It was reported that an SF Express delivery man had scraped a vehicle while collecting parcels in a community named Fugui Garden. The car driver, wearing a black T-shirt, then beat the young delivery man while shouting and cursing. In the video, the delivery man was slapped in the face six times. The young man not only bore this cursing and never fought back but had also voluntarily apologized to the driver. Hearing the apology, the driver said with discontent, "Just sorry?" Then he threatened the young man and asked him to pay for repairs of his own car.

After the video went viral, if one searched keywords such as "SF courier being slapped" or "delivery boy" on Sina Weibo, thousands of relevant posts would pop up. The numbers of reposts and comments reached tens of thousands.

Li Xiang, founder of the vehicle website Autohome, commented: "I'll pay for the repairs, and I'll compensate for his loss of work due to delay" (the man in the black T-shirt was a taxi driver). "But I'll do it with a reasonable requirement – to slap him back for every slap he gave the delivery guy. That's my real wish."

In response to the incident, SF Express's official account stated on Weibo:

> *Most of our delivery men are young lads in their twenties. All year round, whether in wind or rain, they travel across streets and through alleys. They serve with smiles no matter how tired and exhausted they are. We sincerely hope that people can respect and understand each other when accidents happen. We have found the wronged young man and will take good care of him. Don't worry!*

The courier, whose surname was Feng, was a 28-year-old from Hebei Province. He had been working at SF Express for more than six months. After the incident, the staff of SF Express took him to hospital for a physical examination, and got the result that Feng had a soft tissue contusion. Then the staff members left the hospital and went to the local police station in Donghuashi to report the case.

That night, Wang posted on Moments: "If I fail to get justice for my guy, I will no longer deserve to be the president of SF Express!"

Immediately after the founder's tough response, SF Express Group issued a solemn statement:

> *If similar incidents ever happen again, SF Express will protect its rights in accordance with the law, and firmly protect the legitimate rights and interests of its employees. People in the service industry are laborious, so mutual understanding and respect are needed. Hopefully we will all take this as a lesson to uphold fairness and justice in our society.*

SF Express's fight for the rights and interests of couriers was so impressive that it undoubtedly left an imprint on the history of contemporary Chinese enterprises, and it provided an epochal example for current entrepreneurs of how to protect their employees' rights. Of course, the reason why Wang took such a tough attitude was related to his hard experience as a founder, a captain and a courier. Wang has not forgotten the difficult years when he first started his own business and struggled for success.

NOTHING BUT SPEED AND SERVICE

In any era, opportunities are bound to attract people's attention and may bring about fierce competition. This is true of the express delivery industry. As soon as Wang noticed the potential market for express delivery, other people also wanted to give it a try. There were lots of itinerant traders prior to Wang, hoping to gain a lion's share of the industry.

Wang knew clearly that only by doing better and acting faster than these predecessors could he beat them. Otherwise, he would be defeated. Aiming to survive to become the last standing, Wang and his colleagues needed to follow the law of the jungle and actively participate in the bloody scramble. Especially when they squeezed out the profit margins of the emerging itinerant traders, a radical counter-attack awaited them.

Even in 2015, itinerant traders still existed. According to the *Guangzhou Daily*, on 11 January 2015, at the entry hall of Shenzhen's Futian Port, a male passenger wearing a red sweatshirt and black sweatpants drew the attention of customs officers. The passenger's carry-on luggage was too simple: he had only two plastic shopping bags, which were quite different from those of other passengers. Later, the passenger entered the customs corridor with the flow of people, walking at a normal pace, and everything seemed to be fine.

Nevertheless, customs officers soon found that the passenger's walking posture was a little strange – not as fast and natural as others'. He moved stiffly with tensed muscles, and each step made it appear as if he was carrying a heavy weight. Not only that, his facial expression was not natural, and he intentionally avoided any eye contact with customs officers.

Therefore, officers stopped him for a routine inspection. After the passenger took off his coat, dozens of iPhones were found wrapped around his chest, abdomen and legs. He was smuggling 94 iPhones worth more than ¥300,000 in total – a shocking number. Subsequently, officers obtained the passenger's entry and exit records, which showed that he had previously been captured several times for smuggling illegal articles.

The number of itinerant traders was huge, but their illegal operation and their deficiency in fulfilling their deliveries in a timely manner made them lag behind Wang Wei. Finally, they were driven off the central stage of economic history. Although there were still people joining the itinerant traders and perpetuating the old way, their existence was no longer a threat to SF Express.

Meanwhile, hundreds of express delivery companies were springing up in the Pearl River Delta region. At this stage, Wang would encounter incessant expansion while being engaged in a life-and-death battle. Survival was the first issue for SF Express at that time.

In Wang's opinion, if SF Express wanted to survive, it needed to strive for faster deliveries and better service, to establish market barriers and to rebuild core market advantages. And, to remain invincible, a low price was necessary.

While his rivals charged ¥70 for a delivery, he asked for only ¥40. The competitive strategy of charging a low price played a role in SF Express's superiority. In a short period of time, SF Express gained a large number of customers, and even extended its boundaries to the entire Pearl River Delta region.

As a result of Wang's opening up of the express delivery market, the once desolate Portland Street also experienced a revival, leading to an unprecedented amount of activity. Years later, Wang's neighbours still remember it vividly: "Previously, there had been few people in this street. After he came, there were cars picking up goods. Slowly, there were other companies and other stores here. He led the whole street to prosperity."

TEMPORARY VICTORY

In 1996, the SF Express team, led by Wang, won an initial temporary victory. It not only excelled in competition with many express companies but also monopolized the whole of the Shenzhen–Hong Kong freight transportation process, and even won 70% of the market share in the delivery industry in this region at that time.

The rapid development of SF Express posed a threat to its opponents to such an extent that they disparaged SF Express as a 'rat club' (a local term for a kind of Ponzi scheme). Because the staff at SF Express were so busy, they, even Wang himself, had to do packing work late into the night every day. Wang's room, located in a small street at Shunde, glowed with yellow light all night, as people were busy there working like rats foraging for food.

In addition, during the initial stage of SF Express's development, the company didn't have a unified logo or company uniforms. The couriers wore varied clothes. The same was true of the vehicles they used, including trucks and motorcycles, and some even walked on foot. Due to the lack of a proper enterprise management system, it was perfectly appropriate for SF Express to be likened by its competitors to a nest of disordered 'rats.'

Yet this was the epitome of SF Express in the pioneering stage, and it also represented the whole express industry at that time. Facing this problem, Wang took advantage of the situation, decided upon several key points and eventually put the business on a standardized track.

To break the bottleneck of SF Express's development, Wang established a procedure for customs clearance. With the opening-up and improvement of the central government's policies, SF Express was given more opportunities. However, Wang did not remain content with a disorganized 'carry-on' delivery service. Instead, he had parcels gathered and packaged in a standardized form, and gradually created a systematic mode of express operation.

Within a few years of exploration and operation, Wang, less than 25 years old, had grown from the owner of a printing and dyeing factory and an itinerant trader to the leading entrepreneur of the Shenzhen–Hong Kong express delivery industry, with wealth amounting to millions of yuan. However, he was still not content. He was planning the strategic layout of his company for the future.

FOCUSING ON THE MIDDLE AND HIGH-END MARKETS

For any entrepreneur, achieving the desired effect in a commercial competition means exceeding the expectations of customers.

Wang Wei believes that in a competition the trump card is by no means low pricing or vying for customers at all costs and with every means at one's disposal. Instead, it is continually elevating standards to meet customers' expectations. Once customers feel satisfied with the services a company provides, prevailing over one's rivals will just be a matter of time.

Wang Wei once said:

> *When we talk about catching up with international champion express enterprises, in what aspects should we catch up with them? First of all, I think, it is not a matter of scale, but the quality of their service, their popularity, and their pursuit of consumers' recognition and social respect. Secondly, it is necessary to evaluate our own capacity to realize such a goal. Construction on a shaky foundation is most likely to end up with an unstable building, or even with disaster. We need to make a clear assessment of ourselves and to advance with a steady pace. As for how fast we can go, or how far we can forward our steps, there's no necessity to make any excessive demands. Thirdly, most of our efforts depend on the sustaining stability of our national industrial policy.*

Bearing this in mind, Wang had diverted his business from printing and dyeing to delivery. Then, with his service attitude and the guideline of 'the customer as the centre,' he stood out in the field of delivery.

When SF Express grew to a certain size, Wang began to cast his sights on a real giant in the express delivery industry – FedEx Corp, whose headquarters are in Tennessee in the United States.

As is widely known, FedEx is a multinational enterprise that owns abundant funds and has a superlative management mechanism. FedEx, as an international express group, provides services such as overnight delivery, ground delivery, heavy cargo express, document copying and logistics services. Impressed by its professional operation, Wang benchmarked his company against FedEx, and even took FedEx as his model.

After conducting further study, Wang found that, rather than involving itself in all businesses at the start-up stage, FedEx had been selective in providing express services, focusing on small parcel delivery. The reason was that delivering small parcels (such as plasma, organs, medicines and important documents) required not only speed but also a restricted range of efficient delivery modes. At that time, FedEx chose to cover only five cities that were geographically close to each other.

This showcased how FedEx stepped into the market. Consequently, it accumulated a good reputation for its ability to provide relevant services and laid a solid foundation for its later development on a large scale.

Wang was inspired by FedEx's strategy of blue ocean expansion.[11] So, as soon as SF Express grew to a certain scale, it began to collect only certain types of parcels, which was quite different from the strategy of other enterprises, which would accept all orders.

Wang held that SF Express should aim at the middle and high-end markets, providing customers with the highest level of service. What's more, the weight of a parcel needed to be properly limited.

It is worth mentioning that the rise of e-commerce centred around Taobao, an online trading platform, has brought unprecedented opportunities to the express industry in China, where the number of online shoppers is immense.

Statistics show that the number of deliveries from Taobao can reach several million per day. On 11 November 2018, 1 billion orders were placed on Taobao. Data reveals that in 2018, the Tmall Double 11 Global Shopping Festival achieved a turnover of more than ¥200 billion. Meanwhile, the volume of parcels sent as a result of these orders on the day reached over 1 billion, setting a new record and ushering China into a new era of transporting a billion parcels a day.[12]

Faced with the huge market for e-commerce express, some express enterprises, including the 'Four TOs' (namely HTO Express, STO Express, YTO Express and ZTO Express) and Yunda Express, began to set foot in the e-commerce express business. The competition in the field led to a price war. According to statistics, at one point, Taobao's express delivery business accounted for about 70% of the total business of the above-mentioned five express companies.

Wang's belief that SF Express should firmly focus on the middle and high-end markets explains why it did not expand its business on Taobao. In the middle and high-end markets, providing customers with high-quality services and thus getting their approval should be considered the priority.

In an interview on CCTV-2 (the financial channel of China Central Television), Wang stated:

> *I think, in the future, we should put customers' experience in first place, and then speed. This should be the right order, rather than putting the undying pursuit for speed before customer experience.*
>
> *Today we need to redefine the word 'speed,' and completely base it on the customer experience. In other words, even before customers ask for better services, we should have already made plans to upgrade*

our entire service and management system to ensure a close interaction with our customers. At the same time, such interaction is maintained backstage, not by humans but by AI, which can integrate all the service resources to serve a client through only one instruction. Therefore, we don't need human labour to do this job any more, because it will slow down the speed in the future. My real thought is, this is a competence that a delivery company should have in the next era.

These later remarks represented Wang's business concept at the start of SF Express. Wang believed that for SF Express, the essence of business competition was not to vie for customers but to improve its services and better serve its customers.

Once SF had satisfied its customers, it was only a matter of time before it would win the competition in the industry. With the growth of its reputation, SF Express became a reputable brand name, helping thousands of online shops to attract buyers. As a result, these shops actively sought cooperation with SF Express, and even emphasized "Delivered by SF Express" on their homepages.

When the time was ripe, Wang decided to march toward the e-commerce express market. He declared in a speech to his employees in 2013:

SF Express has reached today's position by following a differentiated competitive strategy. We are different from other express companies in services and market positioning. At the same time, we would like to send a clear message to our customers – the express services SF Express provides are fundamentally different from others.

CHAPTER 2

A SHIFT FROM FRANCHISING TO REGULAR CHAINS, COUPLED WITH INTERNAL MANAGERIAL PROMOTIONS

Our rivals in the oncoming cross-industrial competition will be ... IT companies. The essence of such competition is to win in the field of technology, especially in recruiting technological talents. You can never vie with technology companies without sufficient resources in the form of talents.

– Wang Wei

FROM THE FRANCHISE MODE TO REGULAR CHAINS

By 1996, under the guidance of Wang Wei, SF Express had almost monopolized the express delivery business between Hong Kong and the mainland, becoming a de facto hidden champion of the industry. At that time, with its coverage encompassing the whole South China market, SF Express's business volume had nearly surpassed that of all its rivals.

Having consolidated his gains in this portion of the national market, Wang had to face a new task that would decide the destiny of both himself and his company: whether SF Express, which was already a top player in Guangdong, should remain in its comfort zone as a regional baron or expand its corporate frontiers into other regions.

In the specialized field of delivery, some major companies, especially Best Express, STO Express, YTO Express, Yunda Express and ZTO Express, were destined to rely on the franchise mode to expand their business. This was because the advantages of this mode (as seen in the expansion stage of a business) outweighed its disadvantages.

At this time, SF Express, while gathering momentum like a crouching South China tiger, started to expand its territory in line with Wang's scrupulous planning. Like most express delivery companies, SF Express initially chose the mode of franchising. But Wang was subsequently woken up by a complaint call, and he realized that overexpansion of franchising might result in an unimaginable crisis for SF Express. To avoid this, SF Express finally started its strategic transformation – a long journey from franchising to the mode of regular chains.

FRANCHISING: THE INITIAL STAGE OF EXPANSION

During the earliest expansion stage of SF Express, any advancement of its business frontiers meant tapping into a national-scale express delivery market. At that time, the management of SF Express found it hard to reach any consensus on the issue and had to hold an internal debate. The moderates believed that SF Express should keep on consolidating the market of South China. Such a strategy would not only guarantee sufficient business volume and high profits but would also protect the company from fierce battles with other companies in the new markets. According to the moderates, it was better to grow steadily than to participate in riskier regions of competition.

To expand or to stand fast: it is a question that many Chinese enterprises have to face. Generally, the founders of start-up companies trust that, when their companies have achieved a certain size, more aggressive financial advancement will be needed to enact the strategy. Their reasoning is that the huge niche market in China, or the 'blue oceans,' will become a source of profit to facilitate the cash flow required in the future.

Wang was inclined toward such ideas at first. In his view, although there was a lack of strategic resources (such as personnel and adequate financial support) for his three-year-old company, he was confident in the market potential of China. In the 1990s, especially after Deng Xiaoping's Southern Inspection Tour speeches, China was witnessing a boom of entrepreneurship. Whoever first started a new venture could seize a huge opportunity, with associated risks and profits.

However, in the underdeveloped financial market at the time, venture capital was rarely heard of in China. The possibility of any express delivery enterprise getting venture capital was almost zero, and even getting a bank loan was unlikely. Wang knew that the cash assets he had accumulated were far from enough to support any large-scale expansion across China. However, he also realized that, while SF Express did not have the necessary support of external funds, neither did its rivals.

Faced with such an alluring blue ocean in the market, Wang made up his mind to expand tentatively, on a rather small scale. He soon declared that SF Express would accrue money from inside, since gaining the support of external funds was impossible.

To seize the opportunity, it was necessary to expand beyond Guangdong into a nationwide market against all the odds. According to Wang's overall strategy, it was wisest to grab the market share in the Yangtze River Delta Economic Zone (including Jiangsu, Shanghai and Zhejiang), instead of making an all-out assault. Wang's choice was based on the fact that the Yangtze region had the highest economic growth rate, the largest economic size and the greatest development potential of all regions since the start of China's reform and opening-up in the 1980s.

In the delivery market, there was a popular saying that "whoever dominates the East China market takes all." Although there was no convincing evidence behind this statement, such a saying indicated the importance of the Yangtze region for SF Express's national strategic layout. Since "whoever dominates the East China market takes all" was an open secret, it was understandable that Wang needed to prepare especially carefully to win his battle in this area. To occupy a new market is no less difficult than extracting teeth from a tiger's mouth, which means SF Express had to play its own game, with a scenario much more complicated than that required in the Pearl River Delta.

This movement had actually been decided by a pressing situation back in 1993. At the same time that Wang opened a branch in Hong Kong's Longlan Street, Nie Tengfei and Zhan Jisheng, who came from Tonglu in Zhejiang Province, co-founded Shentong Freight Forwarding Co Ltd (STO Express) in Hangzhou. The latter's main business was to send declaration forms for trading companies from Hangzhou to Shanghai by overnight delivery. In 1995, after two years of rapid development, STO Express had successively expanded its market from Hangzhou to Ningbo, Jinhua and Dongyang. In 1996, the network of STO Express extended to Nanjing and Suzhou in Jiangsu Province. In 1997, after several years of growth, it was on a steady track of ascendance, opening branches in Beijing, Chengdu, Guangzhou, Qingdao, Wuhan and other cities. By 1998, the five-year-old STO Express already possessed more than 50 service branches, mainly in the Yangtze River Delta region.

Under the circumstances, the 'Tonglu Circle' headed by STO Express presented one of the biggest obstacles to SF Express's attempts to expand into the East China market. However, further research showed that, in spite of the existence of so many delivery enterprises, what was lacking was a highly qualified service, owing to the prevalence of down-pricing competition and extremely chaotic manoeuvres.

In order to make good use of such a situation, SF Express adopted a combination of low price and a high-quality service, which had proved successful in the Guangdong market. However, what was neglected was that SF Express's business operation was mainly based on setting up regular chains, and this model faced new challenges when it was replicated in the East China market.

Compared with Guangdong, the East China market was of a much larger size. That meant SF Express needed to invest enough funds over a short duration to establish a large number of chain depots. Therefore, it had no alternative but to duplicate the existent franchising model.

During that time, SF Express would set up a subsidiary company for every chain depot. So the network across the Yangtze River Delta differed from the previous one in the Pearl River Delta. It did succeed in laying an early foundation for SF Express in the new area. However, in this business expansion, the drawbacks of the franchise model were quite obvious, in spite of the fact it enabled SF Express to quickly break into the East China market.

Nevertheless, with the snowball effect of franchising, SF Express subsequently conquered the delivery market in both Central China and North China, attaining a period of high-speed expansion.

When SF Express took its stand in the markets of South, East, Central and North China, it had completed the construction of a delivery network that covered most parts of China. For Wang, the reason why SF Express was able to embrace the new opportunity for high-speed development was this series of bold manoeuvres – an aggressive financial expansion strategy that had been scheduled years ago.

After several rounds of adjustment, especially after 1999, SF Express smoothly sailed into the waters of steady growth, and was expected to be a hidden champion among China's private-owned delivery enterprises.

SWITCHING TO THE MODE OF REGULAR CHAINS

Then, in 1999, despite the rapid development of SF Express, Wang was confronted with the problem of choosing the direction in which SF Express should advance. Nowadays, most researchers agree that 1999 should be regarded as the turning point of the company.

At this time, numerous internet companies were springing up like mushrooms across China. In early 1999, Wang Juntao founded a website named 8848, marking the birth of the first e-commerce website in China. Thereafter, Wang Juntao was called "the father of China's e-commerce." In September 1999, Jack Ma retreated from Beijing to a 150-square-metre house in the community of Lakeview City in Hangzhou, where he co-founded Alibaba with his 18 partners, nicknamed the '18 Arhats.' In November 1999, Dangdang, the Chinese version of Amazon, was founded by Li Guoqing and Yu Yu, marking the first e-commerce platform to sell books on the internet in China. Thus, a series of commercial legends started one by one.

From a sociological perspective, many entrepreneurs, professors and researchers regard 1999 as 'Year Zero' for e-commerce in China. With the ebbs and flows of time, there have been a number of ambitious entrepreneurs who have lost out in fierce competitions and had to withdraw from the arena. Nevertheless, there have emerged such e-commerce giants as Alibaba, which has prospered ever since and, on 11 November 2018, achieved an amazing daily transaction total of ¥213.5 billion in a single day.

Yet, for many start-ups, the disadvantages they had to live with remained unchanged. That is why, with stable growth in Guangdong that had helped it to become the local hidden champion, SF Express still chose to establish its delivery branches in the form of franchising.

With five or six years of expansion beyond its market in Guangdong, and strategic arrangements from a national perspective, SF Express seemed to be steadily continuing in the franchise mode. But then Wang Wei received a complaint phone call, which urged him to make a change. Through the complaint call, Wang realized the negative effects of the franchise system. Although, previously, Wang had heard some negative things about the franchise mode, he had not been alerted to the severity of the situation. For him, this complaint call was no less than a warning that it was high time to strengthen the company's corporate management. Following this line of thought, Wang put in place a series of new regulations and measures, but they did not quite solve the problems the company was facing. So, he had to reconsider the whole system and come up with a new model of corporate management.

After careful consideration, Wang decided that in order to solve the problems that SF Express was encountering, it was necessary to carry out a thorough reform to transfer the franchise system to the mode of regular chains. The reason for implementing this reform was that, though franchising had played an important role in the growth of SF Express, it had many disadvantages as well. For example, under this mode, the relationship between headquarters and the branches was relatively loose, and sometimes the branches would disagree with or even refuse to apply the management policies made by headquarters.

The deficiency in implementing management policies made it difficult to ensure the anticipated quality of services. And in their routine services, some franchised network branches even made unauthorized moves to integrate business from other fields to pursue their own interests. With some franchise members operating for their own convenience, a segregated and inefficient mode of management was sure to follow.

In Wang's view, to solve the dilemma, he needed to be as decisive as the legendary figure in a Chinese vernacular novel who cut off his right arm for a grander cause. As SF Express aspired to be a great international delivery company, it was especially necessary to ensure the precise execution of its managerial institutions. Thus, the mode of regular chains was a feasible choice for SF Express. The reason was that the mode would put an end to the disorder by standardizing the management of the franchised service depots all over the country.

Wang believed that only the mode of regular chains could improve the company's overall service level. However, it would undoubtedly take much effort to make the transition.

Years later, Wang recalled that:

> *With the proposal of differentiated management, SF Express encountered a lot of trouble in the transition. At that time, a franchised service branch was like a small kingdom, exerting great pressure against our efforts to eradicate these problems.*

Wang recognized that the disadvantages of the franchise mode had been hindering SF Express from becoming bigger and stronger, since the franchised branches were like separate dukedoms that were both insular and unresponsive to orders from headquarters.

To break the deadlock, the franchise mode needed to be completely abolished. When this strategic decision was put on the agenda, it was naturally met with opposition. Yet Wang was so determined that he not only held his ground against all dissenting views but also continued on with the redesigned policies and boldly streamlined the previous mode of management. Because this reform would certainly act against the interests of individual branches, some of them even joined together to resist the new policy. They intended to send Wang a message saying that, in the coming days, none of his strategic decisions would be followed beyond the sphere of his chairman's office, so as to make him retreat in the face of such difficulties.

Understandably, such turbulence was not easily pacified. It has been said that Wang's opponents were so furious that he was even physically threatened. He responded by hiring bodyguards, both to protect himself and to ensure the smooth progress of the new mode. To this day, whenever Wang goes out, he still has the habit of keeping bodyguards around him.

Even with his insistence on the need for the change, it was not until 2002 that SF Express had completed its transition. This signified Wang's victory in reclaiming the right of corporate governance. Wang held that making profits was the fundamental purpose of running a business. But the problem was that, driven by mere profits, the franchised branches were getting into an ever-worsening situation of chaotic management.

In 2002, in order to adjust the course of the company, Wang sold some of his own properties to buy back management voting shares from the franchised branches, transforming the management mode to that of a regular chain. It was a wise move to reclaim the administrative power by taking direct control, and this became a key to SF Express's growth into a real giant. This strategic transition could be regarded as one of the most significant turning points in the history of SF Express's development. As soon as the reform was complete, Wang firmly regained dominance in regulating all of the branches, which meant that any instruction issued from headquarters had to be implemented by all.

THE PERFORMANCE MEASUREMENT MECHANISM

For any enterprise that has grown to a considerable size, what is needed is a standardized set of management procedures. When it comes to employee management, every entrepreneur has their own means and methods, and some will even resort to rather harsh regulations and fines to boost morale.

But Wang Wei has his own standards of judgement. As a leader who used to be a front-line worker, he has a deep understanding of all the difficulties and hardships that a courier has to face, hence he formulated a mechanism based on points deduction to replace charging fines. This mechanism was mostly welcomed by his employees, though there have been some disputes around it.

STANDARDS OF DELIVERY

Among the various news stories about the delivery industry, one has drawn many people's attention: Wang Wei once spent ¥100 million on customized apparel from Nike for his employees.

It is said that each set of clothes, worth over ¥2,000, was from the Nike Shield series and featured several fancy technologies. For example, reflective strips were stitched on both shoulders of the garment, enabling other drivers and pedestrians to quickly notice the presence of the wearer, which would help to guarantee couriers' safety. Such clothing was also windproof, waterproof, breathable, lightweight and suitable for severe weather.

This action immediately caused a sensation, as well as wide media coverage. For example, the *Southern Metropolis Daily* reported as follows:

> *SF Express has recently teamed up with Nike to launch a line of apparel for SF couriers, which is windproof, waterproof and lightweight. Of course, if the purchase can get Nike's manufacturers to choose SF Express as their future partner for logistic services, no one can deny it is a good cooperation.*

The first group of newly dressed couriers were from East China, including Shanghai. They were followed by SF Express couriers in other regions. Wang explained that the ventilation of the old uniforms had been rather poor; thus, they would easily stick to the sweating bodies of couriers in the hot summer months, leaving an untidy impression that was detrimental to the image of SF Express as a high-end service provider.

Certainly, there was another deeper reason for the new uniforms: after Wang chose the operational mode of regular chains, what he most valued was its efficient implementation of administrative decisions. The change of working uniforms was an early example of such a decision.

In Wang's view, SF Express should give its employees a sense of pride and honour. One media report in *Chinese and Foreign Management* featured one of the company's employees, Mr W, a courier born in the 1990s. He admitted that what had most attracted him to join the company was its high salary, its professionalism and its wide influence. What he had not expected was that, to be a qualified courier, he needed to not only strictly abide by rules and regulations but also meet various performance indicators, such as member registrations and amount of parcel insurance. In spite of these strict requirements, Mr W felt proud of himself, especially when he was rewarded by SF Express for having signed a substantial delivery contract.[13]

It is true that, though the daily work of couriers such as Mr W is utterly exhausting, it can bring them a sense of pride. There are innumerable similar cases, which explains why the employee turnover rate of SF Express is less than 30%, while that of the whole industry can be as high as 70% on average.

Besides the high salary, the success of SF Express in retaining its employees is due to the management mechanism of regular chains. That is why SF Express has become a benchmark for the whole industry.

DEDUCTION OF PERFORMANCE POINTS: A DEVICE BETTER THAN LEVYING FINES

Any set of management policies naturally places restraints on the behaviours of employees, which Mr W fully understands. One time, his "rough handling of packages" was recorded in detail by the delivery depot's monitoring system. Later he was penalized with a deduction of three performance points. As an experienced worker, he knew very well that any rough handling, if detected, would lead to severe punishment, so up to that point he had always paid close attention to his handling practices.[14]

However, this time he was punished for improper operation. Mr W explained that he had dropped a package to the ground from no higher than his ankle (when a package is dropped, the standard distance between it and the contact surface should be no more than 30 centimetres). Nevertheless, Mr W's action was deemed a violation of regulations.

Mr W then went to the person in charge of the delivery depot, wishing to clarify the situation. The manager helped him to review the monitoring records and expressed his regret that he could do nothing to reverse the decision. Such deductions of performance points can be very serious. Mr W was quite upset, for he didn't know how long it would take him to make up for the three lost points.

Readers may wonder why SF Express's couriers should attach so much importance to their performance points. That is because, whenever they violate any regulation, the deduction of performance points is the most severe punishment, much severer than the levying of a fine. Every employee of SF Express initially has 20 performance points. If they violate any of the company's regulations and have points deducted, they lose the opportunity for future promotion. Therefore, when it comes to the process of internal promotion, performance points are an indispensable criterion for evaluation. If an employee's performance points go below ten, they have to worry about the prospect of being dismissed. If all 20 points have been deducted, SF Express will automatically terminate the labour contract.

Usually, it is difficult to reclaim points once they have been deducted. However, there are several ways to add to the total points, such as dispatching an international express delivery.

There are plenty of cases similar to Mr W's at SF Express. For example, the penalty for any employee who shows a bad attitude to customers is a five-point deduction. Even if the customer was in a bad mood and issued a groundless complaint against a specific courier, the courier would have to accept the punishment of point deduction.

In Wang's view, no one, including himself, can cross the 'three red lines,' which are intolerance of poor service attitude, loss of delivered goods, and violation of established rules and regulations. Therefore, whoever in SF Express dares to commit such breaches will face a deduction of performance points at best and a dismissal at worst.

Of course, administrative staff are also punished equivalently to front-line couriers, because of their joint responsibilities. For example, if an administrative staff member fails to ask the customer to register their real name for delivery, the penalties are as follows: deduction of performance points, immediate suspension of work and confiscation of the handheld terminal (barcode scanner). After this, the related delivery depot supervisor, branch manager and branch supervisor will be sanctioned, and performance points will be be deducted accordingly.

In contrast with other major delivery companies (such as STO Express, YTO Express, Yunda Express and ZTO Express), which use fines to regulate their employees, SF Express almost never resorts to the fining of its employees. According to Wang, the reasons for the exclusion of such punitive means are as follows. First, from his own experience, he sympathizes with the front-line couriers and knows the hardships and difficulties they face. Second, he believes that there are many other measures that are more effective than levying fines. Comparatively, those incentive measures can better solve employees' problems with violating regulations. Third, in addition to deducting performance points for employees' violation of regulations, the company correspondingly provides necessary training aids or makes adjustments to depots.

According to *Chinese and Foreign Management*, Xiao Bei, a courier from YTO Express, said in an interview that he had for a long time processed deliveries in the same region with another courier, from SF Express. "He [the courier from SF Express] disappeared several times," joked Xiao Bei. "After a few days, he would reappear, telling me that he had been asked to get retrained for accepting prohibited goods. Yet soon after, I found he 'disappeared' again."

With regard to this kind of suspension, Mr W explained in the interview with *Chinese and Foreign Management*: "As long as there are complaints, the employees involved should cease their work and go directly to Shunyi District for retraining."[15]

In order to establish more effective vocational training, SF Express has purchased several professional training companies. If a courier is disciplined but still fails to be aware of the severity of their misconduct and repeatedly touches the red lines set by the company, or if their performance continuously declines, then they are likely to be transferred to other posts, even to communities with much smaller workloads. For the courier, this means a reduction of wages. So they are obliged to make their own choice: either fully perform their duties to win an internal promotion, or quit their job and leave the company.

This performance evaluation mechanism has aroused much dispute. In the aforementioned article in *Chinese and Foreign Management*, Mr Z, a former senior executive of SF Express, commented that the core of the company's efficiency and service quality control was a "ruthless" evaluation mechanism, which required its employees to be fully responsible for the consequences, sometimes even regardless of factors beyond human control.[16]

A BALANCE BETWEEN FAIRNESS AND HIGH INCOME

Although SF Express adheres to a rigorous appraisal system, it pays far higher salaries than its rivals. *Chinese and Foreign Management* reported that a SF Express courier whose service area covered several communities around the China World Trade Center in Beijing once gained a wide notoriety for his high salary: ¥120,000 per month for two consecutive months.[17] What is special here is that, being overburdened with his routine collections and distributions, the courier asked several of his relatives to deliver for him.

According to the company's corporate design, SF Express couriers' income falls into three categories: A, B and C. Usually the four cities of Beijing, Guangzhou, Shanghai and Shenzhen are considered A-level areas, as the average monthly income of a courier in such areas can exceed ¥15,000. In such areas, while trying hard to keep couriers' income high, SF Express seeks to ensure equilibrium and fairness in income distribution by using its flexible adjustment system. For example, the above-mentioned courier with a monthly salary of ¥120,000 was obviously a rare exception. Such an unreasonable disparity between this single case and the average was soon reduced by adjusting the operation system in this specific area.

According to Mr Z, the aforementioned former senior executive of SF Express, there are three types of terminal collection and dispatching system:

1. Direct delivery to customers
2. Relay delivery, in which three or four couriers collaborate to collect and deliver packages across a broad area and share the gains
3. Transit delivery, where in a certain area, a shuttle truck connects regular deliveries at different posts[18]

In order to balance the monthly salaries of all couriers, when the amount of a courier's piece work reaches a certain number, SF Express will adjust the collection and dispatching structure in the area according to the specific situation. Sometimes more couriers will be sent to the service area so as to even out the unbalanced workload.

When the number of couriers increases in a service area, people will try every means possible to develop potential customers, so as to increase their work volume and corresponding salaries. Thus, apart from their routine work of collection and delivery, couriers voluntarily participate in the task of business development.

As is commonly known, depot managers are usually those responsible for moving couriers between regions. When a depot is in charge of six to eight collecting and distributing sections, newly employed couriers will be assigned to the sections with relatively smaller work volumes, and experienced ones will gradually be transferred to sections with relatively larger volumes. According to Mr Z, such transferrals are the job of depot managers, whose judgement determines whether it is worthwhile to replace a high-income deliverer with a low-income novice.

The fundamental reason for this management design is that the main assessment criterion for each depot is business revenue. According to Mr Z, "The structure-oriented managerial system may reduce the frequency of irresponsible activities. Any management decisions that contribute to the fulfilment of set objectives should be considered right."[19]

MANAGERIAL PROMOTIONS FROM WITHIN

One of the most commonly known stories about SF Express is that some of its couriers have become professional pilots. "At SF Express, the management echelon is promoted from within," Mr W told *Chinese and Foreign Management*. "Even the cargo pilots are selected from the rank and file."[20]

Many researchers have concluded that such motivational examples could only happen at SF Express. This is because almost all recruitment at SF Express follows the principle of internal priority, which means that when there is a job vacancy at SF Express, employees on every level, from top management to rank and file, will receive this information.

Subsequently, any employee with sufficient qualifications can apply for any position. Through this means of internal selection, any front-line employee can expect to become a deputy director through a series of careful steps.

The result is that depot supervisors and branch managers drawn from front-line couriers through internal selection account for more than 90% of the whole management, and even 60% to 70% of the regional superintendents used to be grass-roots couriers.

Although the express delivery industry is known for its high turnover rate, it is common for SF Express couriers to have worked there for more than ten years. As a result, the company has never lacked inspirational stories. For example, a courier who had not even finished primary school was eventually promoted to the executive position of regional superintendent through internal selection, and has the privilege of direct contact with Wang Wei.

A CLEAR CAREER TRAJECTORY

Wang Wei's favouring of internal promotion is based on six obvious advantages.

First, internal selection is more effective and credible. When it comes to personnel designations for key positions, research on the effectiveness and credibility of different mechanisms shows that internal selection is more objective than other methods. This is because the evaluative data regarding competence and performance can be directly drawn from the in-house human resources department. In addition, most managers already have a good understanding of their staff's personality, working motivations and potential for development.

Second, existing employees may better identify with corporate values. In the management of personnel, one of the most difficult parts is the assimilation of the company's culture. Comparatively, employees who have been working in an enterprise for a long time are more likely to share its values, being more accommodated to the working environment and more cooperative with others.

Third, existing employees may have a better understanding of the enterprise's operational procedures. Thus, they can more readily become accustomed to the new role than newcomers from the outside.

Fourth, existing elite employees, if thus promoted, have more motivation to work for the company. Research shows that internal selection can provide employees with a cherished opportunity for promotion, which will not only make them more motivated but also enhance their loyalty to the company. This is especially true of the selection of senior management personnel, for such a promotion is often followed by a series of promotions in other departments and will certainly boost their morale. It also sets a good example for the company, and through its influence will help to arouse a progressive and aspirational atmosphere at work.

Fifth, it can reduce unnecessary expenditure. From the perspective of enterprise cost management, the internal promotion system can cut down recruitment expenses, such as advertising and travel expenses for recruiters and candidates, together with such unnecessary costs as novice training.

Sixth, there is more satisfaction with the enterprise's existing salary system. Generally speaking, the salary requirements of those who have been promoted from within will be more in line with the enterprise's real requirements, because they are more familiar with the details of the existing system.

Wang Wei is aware that many internally promoted administrators who got their first job at SF Express may not have an educational background that is generally considered satisfactory. Without any higher education, they may face problems such as a lack of professional knowledge, insufficient experience and a limited horizon. To solve this problem, SF Express offers two parallel channels of promotion for employees, namely the administrative line and the professional line.

Wang's intention is obvious. The purpose of recruiting professional managers is to assist existing employees to follow the administrative line. Moreover, professional managers can transfer their specialized knowledge and experience to existing employees and help them to improve.

On the administrative side, the manager in charge of a depot in Beijing (for example) often directs 100 or 200 employees. These managers have been internally promoted and have richer experiences and wider social networks, enabling them to be better communicators with their couriers.

It is through this narrative of internal selection that SF Express continuously conveys a clear message to the grass-roots couriers: as long as they work hard, they will become managers of SF Express at various levels, through a clear-cut and fair assessment and promotion system. In this way, the company offers a very clear trajectory of career development for all couriers. Couriers' direct managers are vivid examples. For an ordinary courier at the bottom of the career ladder, there may be no better way up than to aspire to their manager's position. If they left SF Express, there would be many uncertainties about their future prospects.

There is no denying that SF Express owes its success, to a large extent, to the high loyalty of its employees. Of course, the degree of loyalty often corresponds to their identification with the corporate culture.

At SF Express, besides there being regular training for employees, depot managers often exchange positions with each other, usually for a few months. That is, the manager of Depot A is dispatched to Depot B while the manager of Depot B is sent to Depot C, the one of Depot C to Depot D, and so on. The advantage of regular exchange is that grass-roots couriers' loyalty is not bound to their depot managers, but connected with the enterprise's overall values. In contrast to other major companies, such as STO Express, YTO Express and ZTO Express, this meticulous and strict management system is based on SF Express's mode of using regular chains rather than franchises.[21]

HALF OF EXECUTIVES ARE SELECTED FROM THE GRASS-ROOTS

In some teams within SF Express, almost half of the senior executives are selected from grass-roots staff. The mechanism of internal promotion has actually accelerated the company's development.

The piecework portion of their salary accounts for a large portion of an employee's income at SF Express. This structural design is intended to ensure the high income of front-line employees, and then make it an incentive for them to support the company's high-quality service based on delivery speed.

The base pay of couriers at SF Express is actually not very high. However, the inclusion of a piecework portion in the salary ensures a promising monthly income, as well as high quality of service. What couriers ultimately earn is based on their diligence and customers' satisfaction. As a result, it is not extraordinary for couriers at SF Express to receive monthly pay that surpasses ¥10,000.

Additionally, SF Express also gives subsidies and benefits to its employees' families.

Chen Ping, the former president of ZJS Express, said:

> *Couriers at SF Express are assigned directly by headquarters to each branch, instead of being hired by franchisers. And that's the wisdom of Wang Wei – in reclaiming his decision-making power from the earlier years. He applied different policies toward franchisers and their employees. He would only dismiss those disobedient franchisers, while keeping their employees, as long as they would listen to him. Unexpectedly, the result was very good.*

This comment was verified by a driver who had worked at SF Express for five years and in recent days had become an administrator through its promotion system.

ENHANCING EMPLOYEES' LOYALTY AND PROVIDING A BETTER SERVICE FOR CUSTOMERS

Now that SF Express enjoys a high reputation in the industry, the media and scholars particularly focus on the income and welfare of its front-line couriers. Though it is an open secret, the management of human resources at SF Express is a topic followed by numerous researchers, who try to satisfy the curiosity of outsiders by systematically exploring Wang Wei's strategy.

According to Wang, only when SF Express's employees, especially those on the front line, enjoy an enticing income and an ever-improving working environment can they repay customers with sincerity and a better service. "This is the only way to make our service prices convincing. And then our customers will feel comfortable about our service products," Wang said. "This creates a benign circle and, as a result, I firmly believe that our profits will no longer be a problem."

Such thinking bears a striking resemblance to that of Ren Zhengfei, the founder of Huawei. Ren once said:

> *The reason why Huawei advocates a 'customer-oriented' core value is that Huawei can not live without the support of customers. It is our customers who have been laying the base for the company's development. Any other third party, including the government, would not choose to sustain us with necessary funds for growth. Good services are a prerequisite for our customers to willingly finance our advancement.*

In December 2010, executives from a large European telecommunications company came to Huawei's headquarters in Shenzhen to investigate Huawei's 'customer-oriented' strategy. Ren Zhengfei gave a lecture titled "Customers' Interests, Hard Workers' Welfare and Hard Work."

In his speech Ren explained:

> *Instead of being visionary, this combination of three fundamentals, distilled from our past experience, is Huawei's only secret in surpassing our competitors and winning one victory after another. The trio form an iron triangle and are internally connected and mutually supportive. Among them, 'customers' interests' is our goal of striving in the long run, 'hard work' is the means to cater to customers' interests, and 'hard workers' welfare' is the source of vitality for our striving in the long run – an impetus for catering to customers' interests.*

These three fundamental values are indispensable to Huawei's extraordinary performance. In 2018, Huawei's revenue was US$108.5 billion, with a 21% increase year on year. Guo Ping, the rotating chairman of Huawei, said:

> *Huawei has signed 26 5G commercial contracts with the world's leading operators, and has transported over 10,000 5G base stations all over the world. Among the world's top 500 enterprises in more than 160 cities, 211 have selected Huawei as their partner in digitalized transformation. More than 200 million smartphones have been sold, and welcome breakthroughs were made in the fields of PC business and the Internet of Things smart home ecosystem.*

In the same year, guided by similar principles, SF Express was also acclaimed for its good performance. On 23 August 2018, SF Holding released its 2018 semi-annual report, which contained impressive figures. The financial report showed that in the first half of 2018, SF Holding had achieved a revenue of ¥42.5 billion, up 32.1% year on year, and achieved 60% of its annual target. The net income for shareholders reached ¥2.2 billion, up 18.6% year on year. The number of delivery packages reached almost 1.9 billion, up 35.3% year on year.

Despite the huge differences between SF Express and Huawei, the performance of the former is quite notable. For Wang Wei, the key to SF Express's success is its years of investing in talents. For example, the company even set up 'anger rooms' to enable customer service staff to release their tension. And, many years ago, in order to reduce the pressure on the sorting department, the company spent hundreds of millions of yuan to purchase automatic sorting equipment from abroad.

Wang is always generous to employees, especially to front-line couriers. He often says: "At SF Express, couriers are the most admired. I would rather not call them couriers – I'd like to call them 'kids.'" For Wang, employees are everything, as shown by the story in Chapter 1, where Wang vowed to get justice for an employee who had been slapped by a driver after accidentally scraping the man's car.

In 2016, Wang made only two posts on his WeChat Moments, one of which was the report that the aforementioned courier had been violently assaulted. Deeply moved by their boss, many employees expressed sentiments in interviews such as: "Though I am exhausted every day, I feel very happy here. When you have such a nice boss who both cherishes you and cares about your material needs, what reason do you have not to work diligently?"

In addition to making efforts to improve their loyalty, Wang tries to allow his employees to work with more dignity. Every year, he sets aside a week for himself to carry out delivery work. During the week, Wang rides an electric bike to collect and deliver packages. Each day, he learns more about the application of equipment and materials such as barcode scanners and delivery backpacks, the labour intensity of employees, and the true treatment and working conditions of couriers.

Wang explained:

> *Many of our management often say they are exploring the market, and I tell them, "Put aside the paperwork. What you should think about is how to help employees in the first and the second lines to do a better job of collecting and distributing, and learn about their needs and difficulties at their posts.*

He said:

> *These couriers are at the forefront of market competition and have the most say about the market. If we solve the problems of the first and second lines, the customers' problems will be more readily solved. The result will be that the problem of future development will be mostly solved. This is an industry that is not only motivated by money but also by heart.*

That is why on 24 February 2017, Wang invited the once-bullied delivery man to the company's listing ceremony to ring the bell together.

CHAPTER 3

SPEED IS KING

According to international standards, a 2,000-kilometre freight transport distance is by no means a challenge. But it seems to be so in China. Before my experiment, no one had ever considered air freight for express delivery in China. But it is already common practice in many countries to use aeroplanes or cargo planes for express delivery. So I don't think I have tried something very advanced, or something very cool. No, I don't think so, I just did what others had done.

– Wang Wei

IT'S EXPRESS DELIVERY, NOT SLOW DELIVERY

Wang Wei once pointed out that perfect service, including the speed of delivery, plays a crucial role in winning customers' satisfaction in the express industry. As to the issue of speed, in an interview on CCTV-2, Wang stated:

We should make it clear whether we are talking about a domestic standard or an international one ... Considering the actual situation in China, I have merely tried to do something to pursue my own ideals. I will never offer any service product before I feel satisfied with it. This means it has to be in line with my pursuit of speed. Such things always reflect my own concept of speediness. So, I have kept on seeking more scientific ways, or different modes of transportation, to achieve the goal. There are still gaps between the speediness in my mind, the speediness of my pragmatic goal, and the actual speed I have attained. People might think that

SF Express's delivery is fast compared with its rivals. I myself really don't think we are fast enough.

In Wang's view, a delivery that is not fast should not be called 'express delivery' but 'slow delivery,' and it will hamper a customer's acceptance of the brand.

'EXPRESS' VS. 'SLOW'

By 2002, as explained in Chapter 2, Wang had taken back the administrative power from the franchised branches, turning SF Express into a company based on the mode of regular chains. Moreover, he decided to establish headquarters in Shenzhen, in order to better implement the policies under the new mode.

After the completion of the phased structural change, Wang also began to subdivide the company's target markets, aiming to position his business toward the high-end market of the industry.

In 2003, with the outbreak of SARS (severe acute respiratory syndrome), everyone chose to stay indoors, leaving the streets and alleys empty from day to night. Yet, just as Lao Tzu says in *Tao Te Ching*: "Upon misfortune depends happiness; within happiness hides disaster." A crisis handled properly can become an opportunity.

In the face of this epidemic, entrepreneurs needed to be decisive to take advantage of opportunities. For example, Liu Qiangdong, the founder of JD.com, once said in a media interview that SARS was the first major crisis that JD had suffered. To protect its employees from contracting the disease, he ordered the shutdown of all JD's offline stores, which meant huge losses. In one month, the Zhongguancun store owned by Liu lost as much as ¥1 million.

Without any income from offline stores, JD had to start from scratch to become an e-commerce company. In this way, it inadvertently created a new mode of business, and its present achievements have much to do with the company's adjustments during the SARS crisis.

Like Liu Qiongdong, Wang Wei also found a huge business opportunity during the crisis, which ushered SF Express into a new phase of development. During the SARS period, the airline business plummeted due to a sharp drop in the number of business travellers and tourists. Many airlines had to use price cuts and other promotional measures to boost passengers' enthusiasm for travelling.

Wang saw a business opportunity in the deduction of air freight rates. In early 2003, he signed an agreement with Yangtze River Express and rented five aeroplanes. SF Express thus became the first enterprise to use aeroplanes for delivery in China, which laid a solid foundation for the 'SF speed,' as well as for gaining dominance in the industry.

In addition, Wang made a huge investment to meet the needs of customers, so as to ensure the speed of SF Express.

FUTURE COMPETITORS FROM ANOTHER INDUSTRY

The multinational corporation FedEx saw its Chinese competitors, especially SF Express, as an imminent threat, given their rapid rise. Therefore, it launched a strategy to acquire SF Express. In 2004, FedEx intended to acquire SF Express at a price of ¥5 billion. When the letter of intention was sent to Wang, he resolutely rejected the idea.

In that year, SF Express's volume of business was only ¥1.3 billion, which demonstrates FedEx's strategic vision. For a long time after this, Wang refused to talk about any external capital intervention, so he became regarded as an entrepreneur "who turns his back on every PE [private equity investor] or VC [venture capital investor]." His financial records during the period reveal that SF Express was in fact not as sufficiently funded as it appeared, but Wang knew that capital was like a double-edged sword. Therefore, he chose to turn to the banks for help and tried to get a mortgage of ¥4.2 million on the company's assets from the Bank of China, reportedly for nine times the company's asset value.

This does not mean that Wang is a conservative investor. Instead, it shows the venturous side of his entrepreneurship. It has been said that "Wang Wei is very brave. He has the courage to continuously expand. He will use ¥8 from every ¥10 he has earned to open a new shop." Others frequently say such things about him.

From these two aspects, we can see that Wang has his own strategic judgement about the long journey required for success. He is not only prudent but also visionary – that is, he wants his company to be the 'FedEx of China.'

In order to improve the company's speed of service, Wang has invested much in technology and has even introduced AI technologies into the delivery process. In an interview with CCTV-2, when asked "How can you better improve the speed of service in SF Express?" Wang gave a pragmatic and rational answer:

> *In fact, as you know, big data and AI not only represent a revolutionary change for the logistics industry but for all industries around the world. This revolutionary change is so great that we just cannot predict what will happen in five years: some companies may still exist, some companies may no longer exist,*

and some others may suddenly emerge to control the world.

I've been emphasizing the importance of technology. Now the real competitors we will have to face are definitely not delivery companies or logistics companies. I think our future competitors will absolutely be high-tech companies. The speed of development of the internet and other technologies is so fast that, compared with them, no traditional industry can match the speed of the upgrades.

Wang thinks that, in the future, the dynamics of the express industry will be such that competition will not come from peers but from high-tech companies such as Google. He said: "The core of science and technology is talent. What does SF Express have to attract the top talents?" Wang's concern is not misplaced. Indeed, in the job market, top talents certainly would prefer an outstanding IT company to any IT department of an outstanding company. *Nanfang Daily* once interviewed Wang on this subject. The main topic of the interview was the question "How does SF Express make optimized advancement through technological innovations and talent programmes, so as to provide better services for customers?" Wang answered:

One of the biggest challenges that SF Express faces is the absorption of notions from different perspectives of logistics and technology. In the cross-industry competition in the future, our competitors will be IT companies, and the focus of such competition is technology, among which talent is the core issue. Without talent, competing with these IT companies will be out of the question.

What can SF Express do to create an environment that effectively attracts talent? This is an important question. You can imagine which types of companies these top talents would choose. An IT company like Google and Baidu, or an IT department of companies in other industries? They are likely to choose the former.

Basically, there is only one IT department in a traditional logistics enterprise, which makes it impossible for a traditional enterprise to compete with an IT company. Therefore, it is very important to create a high-tech environment through how the management of the company is structured. This was our original intention in setting up SF Technology.

In 2015, we made another move – merging SF Technology with SF Group, to use high technology to manage SF Express and to allow the technology 'boss' to guide SF Express.

The biggest change brought by this innovative move was the need for the group to nurture its own high-tech incentive mechanism and managerial system, as well as forming a technological culture. We have also employed many tech talents to manage the company.

To be honest, I have a logistics gene myself, but I am an amateur when it comes to IT. I'd like to keep pace with technological innovations, but I do not know the language of the technology circle. So we need to make this big change, to lead the group through technology.

By technologically optimizing the whole corporate system, we are able to reconstruct the old operating procedures and reduce structural costs. For example, our reform in which we furnished call centres with an AI order system spared us 20,000 posts in 2017.[22]

In Wang's view, the purpose of creating a high-tech environment under the new management structure was to effectively improve the speed of service with science and technology. Wang has never been parsimonious regarding technological investment. As early as the end of 2009, the Civil Aviation Administration of China published an announcement that did not attract much attention from other companies. However, this announcement showed to the public an entrant from the express industry with a new profile: the officially approved SF Airlines. That is, SF Group had applied to set up an air route and bought two express planes of its own.

This move marked the first instance of a Chinese private express company having its own cargo planes. By 2011, SF Express already had 150,000 employees, and its volume of business had reached ¥15 billion, with an average annual growth rate of 50% (and a profit margin of 30%).

After more than 20 years, SF Express has achieved rapid development, and this has been inseparable from its tripartite market strategy: use of the mode of regular chains, high-end positioning and air transportation.

STANDARDIZED OPERATING PROCEDURE

Wang Wei thinks that speed is the prerequisite without which express delivery does not exist. Therefore, how to attain 'fast speed' was an urgent requirement for SF Express, especially when the company had finished its shift to the mode of regular chains and the problem of a differentiated market strategy had emerged. With the overall improvement of the company's services, especially with the great leap in service quality, Wang would no longer limit his goal to becoming a giant in China's private express industry. Instead, he intended to make SF Express the 'FedEx of China.'

In order to make SF Express 'fast,' Wang set a relatively clear schedule for the company's development. That is, while specializing in the medium and high-end express markets, the main body of the business should be focused on commercial commodities and be finely segmented.

Years later, Wang explained: "We studied the features of supply chains and pricing of e-commerce, and tried to figure out a better match with our available resources. At the same time, we considered how to improve the added value of our services and customers' satisfaction."

The express industry, at that time, still fell short of standardization. Yet Wang began to put in place a series of standards to quicken the pace of service. He said:

> *One thing that distinguishes SF Express from other express companies is its differentiated strategy of competition. Our delivery services and market positioning are different from those of other express companies. ... In this industry, it is so important to win a good reputation and enough market satisfaction.*

Liu Zhize and Zhang Lüqing wrote in their expert research that "SF Express serves with a standardized operation system – for example, its couriers will pick up parcels within one hour of the order and deliver them nationwide within 36 hours. The company has strict regulations for the front-line couriers and rigorously fulfils its commitment of 'time-definite delivery,' which has shaped a new image for the whole express industry." In the two experts' view, it is SF Express's standardized operating system that has played the essential role. With the full-scale upgrading of China's economy and the boom in e-commerce, the business of SF Express has been significantly boosted.

Under the guidance of Wang, the measures that SF Express took to standardize its operating system worked effectively. Data shows that by 2006, SF Express had become the leading express giant in China, occupying 18% of the market share, especially the lucrative portion of medium and high-end express delivery.

By then, SF Express already had two distribution centres, 52 transit warehouses, more than 2,000 transfer vehicles for the main lines and more than 1,100 service stores in China, forming a huge logistics network that reached everywhere, both at home and abroad. SF Express not only provides distribution-end logistics services but also covers production, supply, sales and distribution at the front end of the value chain. In attending to the needs of customers, it uses big data and cloud computing to provide warehousing management, sales forecasting, big data analysis and settlement management. At the same time, it is already a service provider of intelligent logistics. It has the advantage of scale in its network and is a service provider of comprehensive logistics with a trio of networks – the Aviation Network, the Ground Network and the Information Network – covering numerous cities both at home and abroad.

At the beginning of 2018, the State Post Bureau of China ranked the performance of ten domestic express brands in 2017 on six aspects, including the duration of the whole transport journey, transit time, delivery time and punctuality if completed within 72 hours. The comprehensive ranking of SF Express resulted in it achieving first place among the ten brands (see Chapter 4 for more detail). This amazing achievement from SF Express should be attributed to its standardized operating services, especially its differentiated strategy. And that is why SF Express still stands out in the express industry today.

INCREASING ASSETS AND LOGISTICAL CAPACITY

In order to quicken the steps of the company's express delivery service, Wang Wei sought to expand into an asset-heavy mode of operation. This included the transition to a structure of regular chains rather than franchises (see Chapter 2) and raised doubts in the media about SF Express's high asset–liability ratio.

In January 2018, when the debt of SF Express reached ¥30 billion and its asset–liability ratio increased to 46%, the media and researchers began to pay more attention to the problem of this high asset–liability ratio. Much of the reason for this doubt was that many people did not understand the essence of SF Express's asset-heavy mode. They thought the debt ratio of the company was extremely high compared with those of its A-share peers, such as Yunda Express (33%), YTO Express (31%) and STO Express (19%).

In this regard, Gan Ling, the secretary of SF Holding's board of directors, explained in an interview that the mode of regular chains involves building up heavy assets whereas the franchise mode has light assets. Therefore, the financial data of the companies that use the two modes will naturally differ.

POSITIVE CORRELATION BETWEEN THE ASSET-HEAVY MODE OF REGULAR CHAINS AND THE ASSET–LIABILITY RATIO

The asset–liability ratio is not a new concept for any enterprise. It is expressed as a percentage and is calculated as total liabilities divided by total assets at the end of the accounting period. The formula is as follows:

Asset–liability ratio = total liabilities / total assets

In other words, an enterprise's asset–liability ratio, as a management indicator, reflects the ratio of the capital provided by a company's creditors to all of the company's assets, so it is also called the 'leverage ratio.' When the asset–liability ratio reaches or exceeds 100%, it means an enterprise's net assets are zero and the company is on the verge of insolvency.

Here, we need to clarify two concepts. The first is the total amount of liabilities. An enterprise's total amount of liabilities is the sum of various debts owed by the enterprise, including its current liabilities and long-term liabilities. The second concept is total assets. This refers to the sum of various properties owned by the enterprise, including current assets and long-term assets.

From the definition of the asset–liability ratio, it is not difficult to see that when this ratio is below 100%, it means an enterprise's financial state is relatively safe. The adoption of the asset-heavy mode of regular chains would undoubtedly increase the asset–liability ratio.

To address these questions and doubts from the media, Gan Ling explained:

As the only listed express logistics company based on regular chains in China, SF's assets had reached ¥66 billion by the end of the third quarter of 2018. Compared with the famous direct express enterprises around the world, our debt ratio is still at a low level, as the average debt ratio of the top three international express companies – DHL, FedEx and UPS – is about 70%.

According to Gan Ling, SF Express had been involved in a process of long-term development and would continuously improve its competitiveness and create more value for its shareholders. There is no doubt that the company needed to take a more adventurous attitude in the future.

Data show that the asset–liability ratio of SF Express in January 2019 was 46%, an increase of 3% when compared with 43% at the end of 2017. But the company's financial status was still healthy.

At the same time, SF Express announced that in order to meet the demands of the company's business development at home and abroad, to reduce financing costs and to optimize the debt structure, the board of directors had reviewed and passed a proposal agreeing that the company needed to issue a debt of up to ¥16 billion through its wholly owned subsidiaries Shenzhen SF Taisen Holding (Group) Co Ltd and SF Holding Investment Ltd. The specific details of the issuance were to be decided by the requirements of filing, approval, registration with relevant regulatory bodies and market conditions.[23]

SIGNIFICANCE OF LONG-TERM PLANNING

As we have seen, the asset-heavy mode means that the debt ratio is relatively high, yet it can be maintained within a controllable scope. For this reason, Gan Ling said, "At present, the liquidity of SF Holding is very healthy."

According to *Securities Times*, up to 30 September 2018, the currency capital of SF Holding was ¥10.5 billion. Throughout 2017, its cash flow exceeded ¥120 billion, with a net cash flow of ¥6.1 billion and an interest coverage ratio of 18.1%. At that time, more than ¥60 billion of the company's credit lines remained to be used.[24]

From the data in the *Securities Times* report, we can see that SF Holding was still quite able to obtain funds. Moreover, because of its excellent financial performance in 2018, it was rated by S&P as A-, by Moody's as A3 and by Fitch as A-.

In an interview with *Securities Times*, Gan Ling said:

> *SF greatly values long-term strategic planning and constantly endeavours to strengthen its competitiveness. The changes shown in the financial data are due to some strategic adjustments that are necessary for the short term. In the long run, the financial situation will be more positive and healthier, and we will also repay all kinds of shareholders with more profit.*

Previously, there were some shareholders, such as the company Jiaqiang Shunfeng (Shenzhen), which had reduced their holdings of SF Holding's shares. In Gan Ling's view, in spite of the high debt ratio, the capital was relatively abundant and its financial soundness was evident. Gan said:

> *Shareholders who invested before the company went public are more concerned about the long-term value of their investment. Over the past five years, these shareholders have introduced a lot of high-quality*

business and core talents for us. Now they also highly appreciate SF's long-term strategic plan. Our vision is to become a composite logistics service enterprise driven by new technologies. To this end, we need to strengthen our capacity in technology and supply chain solutions. In 2018, through a series of investment projects, we have integrated many first-rate technology companies and supply chains around the world. In just one year, SF has acquired the ability to find solutions for the industry that normally would have taken years. Thus, SF has made a big step toward its anticipated status as a technology-driven company and is now able to provide its own industry solution services.

Because SF Holding formulated a relatively comprehensive medium and long-term plan, it has been recognized by several long-term funds. Gan said:

According to public information, many well-known investment funds have begun to quietly invest in SF. Apart from domestically well-known private equity funds, there are sovereign funds or top investment institutions from Europe, America, Southeast Asia, the Middle East and other places.

INVESTMENT IN EZHOU AIRPORT HUB

In Wang Wei's view, as mentioned, 'fast speed' is one of the keys to the rapid development of SF. In order to efficiently reinforce the pursuit of speed, SF decided to buy its own express cargo planes. As of 2020, SF Airlines already has 39 all-cargo aircraft.

The air cargo business has added to the competitive edge of SF. Moreover, some preparations for the construction of SF Express airport are now steadily under way. In January 2019, the National Development and Reform Commission (NDRC) of China replied to a feasibility study report on the construction of a new civil airport in Ezhou, Hubei Province. The contents are as follows:

Reply to the Feasibility Study Report on the Project of New Civilian Airport in Ezhou, Hubei Province

National Development and Reform Commission, Department of Basic Industries [2019] No. 53

Development and Reform Commission (DRC) of Hubei Province:

The Proposal of the Feasibility Study Report on the Project of New Civilian Airport *(Hubei Provincial DRC, Department of Transportation [2018] No. 428) and relevant materials you presented have all been received. After our reviewing, the reply is as follows:*

I. In order to implement the national strategies of promoting the development of the Yangtze River Economic Belt, to promote the coordinated development of regional economy and society, to comprehensively improve the regional transportation system, to meet the development needs of air cargo, and to enhance the capacity of emergency response and support, we agree to your plan to construct a new civilian airport in Ezhou.

II. *Main Construction Projects and Their Scale*
In the current project, the runway system and the taxiway system of [the] airfield are designed to meet a passenger traffic of 1.5 million people and a freight traffic of 3.3 million tons in 2030. The terminal area, transit centre and other facilities are designed to meet a passenger traffic of 1 million people and a freight traffic of 2.45 million tons in 2025. The standard for the airfield should be Class 4E. The main construction projects include:
(a) *Airport: Two parallel long-distance runways along the east and west sides, with taxiway systems. The runways will be 3,600 metres long and 45 metres wide, with a distance of 1,900 metres from each other. Precision approach system (Category II) will be installed on the main landing direction, and precision approach system (Category I) will be installed on the secondary landing direction. A terminal of 15,000 square metres, a freight house of 24,000 square metres, and a parking apron of 124 parking bays will be included, together with auxiliary systems of air traffic control, fire rescue, power supply and water supply.*
(b) *Transit Centre and SF Airlines base: The transit centre project includes: A sorting centre of 678,000 square metres, [and] facilities for [the] sorting and transit system. Customs, security checkpoints, SF Airlines offices and spare rooms for auxiliary facilities and equipment, which will total 41,000 square metres.*

The SF Airlines base includes: Aircraft maintenance facilities of 155,000 square metres, ground service facilities of 31,000 square metres, and comprehensive logistics buildings of 198,000 square metres.

(c) *Fuel Supply Project: A fuel depot with a capacity of 40,000 cubic metres, a berth with a tonnage of 5,000, aviation fuel stations and pipelines.*

III. *Total Investment and Sources of Funds*

The total investment of the whole project is ¥32,063 million, consisting of three parts: the airport project, the transit centre and SF Airlines base, and the fuel supply project. The investment of each is as follows:

(a) *¥15.857 billion will be invested in the airport project. The project capital accounts for 50% of the total investment, about ¥7.929 billion. In particular, there will be ¥820 million from the budget of the central government distributed by NDRC [and] ¥1.64 billion from the civil aviation development fund by the Civil Aviation Administration. The rest of [the] ¥5.469 billion will be invested by [the] People's Government of Hubei Province, Shenzhen Nongyin Airport Investment Co., Ltd. and Shenzhen SF Taisen Holdings (Group) Co., Ltd., according to the ratio of 49:5:46, which are respectively 2.68 billion from the public finance of Hubei Province, 273 million from the funds owned by Shenzhen Nongyin Airport Investment Co., Ltd. and 2.516 billion* *from the fund owned by Shenzhen SF Taisen Holdings (Group) Co., Ltd. Funds other than the capital part shall be provided by Hubei International Logistics Airport Co., Ltd., a joint venture established by the three parties, in the form of bank loans.*

(b) The ¥11.529 billion on the transit centre project, and the ¥3.752 billion on the SF Airlines base project, in sum ¥15.281 billion, shall be invested by Shenzhen SF Taisen Holdings (Group) Co., Ltd.

(c) The ¥925 million on the fuel supply project shall be invested by China National Aviation Fuel Supply Co., Ltd.

IV. Hubei International Logistics Co., Ltd., as the legal person for the airport project, Shenzhen SF Taisen Holdings (Group) Co., Ltd., as the legal person for the transit centre and SF Airlines base project, and China National Aviation Fuel Supply Co., Ltd., as the respective legal persons for the airport, transit centre and SF Airlines base, and fuel supply projects, are in charge of the implementation and management of each project.

V. The surveying, designing, engineering and supervision of this project, as well as the procurement of major equipments and materials related to the construction of this project, shall be subject to public bidding. The bidding for the transit centre and SF Airlines base shall be self-organized. Other projects shall be subject to delegated bidding.

VI. *In the follow-up stage, priority should be given to the following works:*
   (a) *Conduct in-depth studies and optimize the regional airspace structure by cooperating with relevant military & civil aviation units; and accelerate the adjustment of both military & civil aviation in the control area, as well as the air route network of Wuhan, so as to optimize the entry and departure procedures of the airport.*
   (b) *Actively prepare for the proposal concerning environment assessment. Coordinate the study of the mode of aircraft operation and noise control, by taking into account the operational characteristics of the airport.*
   (c) *Further optimize the general layout of the airport and strictly control the scale of land used for the project. Implement the plan of farmland subsidy and the measures for forest restoration in accordance with relevant national and local documents. Ensure the arrangement for the emigration of local residents is carried out well.*
   (d) *Further optimize the construction plan of the collecting and distributing network for ground traffic, in accordance with the overall traffic planning of the surrounding area. Promptly implement and raise funds for the construction plans of auxiliary projects around the airport, ensuring that they be concurrently completed with the airport project.*
   (e) *Incorporate the general plan of the airport into the general plan and the land utilization plan*

> *of municipal government, strictly control the use of the surrounding land, and well maintain the required conditions of obstacle clearance and [the] electromagnetic environment, to ensure the safety and normal functioning of the airport.*
>
> *National Development and Reform Commission*
> *January 11, 2019*[25]

The approval means SF Express's dedication to the strategy of speeding up had now paid off. Gan Ling indicated that the sophisticated logistics hub would be essential for SF Express to enhance its advantages in international logistics. As the fourth specialized freight airport in the world and the first in Asia, Ezhou Airport is of great strategic significance to SF Express.

First, there is the pivotal importance of its strategic location. Lying on the southern bank of the middle reaches of the Yangtze River, Ezhou is a prefectural city in eastern Hubei Province. It is an important member of the agglomeration around Wuhan and of the city clusters along the middle reaches of the Yangtze River. At the same time, it is one of the transportation nodes in the eastern Hubei Province.

What Wang Wei values most is that Ezhou Airport is situated in an important strategic location, from which a two-hour flight can reach 90% of the regions of China, which will help to meet middle and high-end customers' needs for timely delivery. In addition, Ezhou has convenient transport networks, including highways, railways, waterways and aviation. The strategy of SF Express is to take the lead in the blue ocean market via multiple means of transportation.

Second, the company's network coverage capacity will be enhanced by Ezhou Airport. When this specialized airport is constructed, SF Express will be able to optimize its hub-and-spoke network with wider coverage, lower costs and higher efficiency, and to give full play to its advantages in speed, stability and range. The company can even expect to build a network of overnight delivery services that covers over 250 cities in China.

Third, the airport will reduce the transport cost for single parcels. The hub-and-spoke network will greatly reduce the demand for air routes paired in opposite directions; therefore, the cost of air transport will drop. Moreover, the transit function of the airport will strongly boost the collection of goods, allowing the company to use larger wide-body aircraft (for example, 757 or 767 Boeing aircraft) to transport goods, which will reduce the transport cost of single parcels.[26]

Fourth, the airport will not only promote the economic development of Ezhou but also create a stable logistics-related demand for the future development of SF Express. While investing in the project, SF Express needs to actively participate in constructing Ezhou Airport and its subports. Working together with Ezhou's government, the company must regard aviation and logistics as interconnected means of developing high-end industries such as medicine, auto and electronic spare parts, and fresh foods. It must also build up relevant storage centres.[27]

Fifth, the project will provide a comprehensive schedule of logistics services. When the airport project is completed, SF Express will add to its catalogue a series of services such as rapid distribution, warehousing, supply chain services, a comprehensive service for bonded goods, import and export, and multimodal transportation. The company today is no longer an express company with a single line of business but an all-channel integrator of logistics solutions, being able to provide customers with comprehensive and diversified services. At the same time, the construction project will also guarantee the smooth growth of the company's business in different segments, such as time-definite delivery, economy delivery, heavy cargo and refrigerated transport.

CHAPTER 4

STRENGTHENING B2B AND CARRYING OUT BOLD INNOVATIONS

SF has been actively improving its capabilities in the field of enterprise services for a long time, and is moving toward the goal of becoming the best integrated logistics solution provider in the eyes of customers. The cooperation with DPDHL Group will enhance the strength of SF's supply chain services in various industries. At the same time, it will enable us to transplant the leading management experience into the operation of supply chain business, and make us a supply chain solution service provider who knows more about customers.

– Wang Wei

DISCOURSE OF THE B-END VOICE

In the evening of 26 October 2018, SF Holding made an impressive announcement. That day, SF Holding Ltd had agreed to establish a strategic cooperation with Deutsche Post DHL Group (DPDHL) in order to further enhance SF Holding's capacity for integrated logistics solutions and improve the strategic layout of its supply chains and contract logistics. According to the agreement, SF Holding would integrate DPDHL's supply chain business in mainland China, Hong Kong and Macao.[28] The transaction did not include other DPDHL businesses in China, such as international express, freight and e-commerce logistics solutions.

With this adjustment, and especially through the two companies' strategic cooperation, SF Holding mainly intended to integrate DHL's supply chain management business, relevant management teams and technology in mainland China, Hong Kong and Macao through mergers and acquisitions. The purpose was to enhance its business-to-business (B2B) competitiveness.

STRENGTHENING B2B

In Wang Wei's view, providing customers with excellent services is the key to the enhancement of competitiveness. In this way, the company would become a hidden champion and win the hearts of numerous customers, plus it would gain official accreditation by the State Post Bureau of China.

At the beginning of 2018, the State Post Bureau issued a list of the top ten whole-network express service brands in China in 2017. The evaluation was based on six aspects: duration of the whole transport journey, processing time at departure, duration of transportation, processing time at the destination, delivery time and rate of punctuality if completed within 72 hours. The overall satisfaction rankings and scores of the enterprises were: SF Express (83.4 points), EMS (79.9 points), ZTO Express (76.8 points), Yunda Express (76.5 points), YTO Express (75.0 points), STO Express (74.1 points), Best Express (74.0 points), ZJS Express (71.9 points), TTK Express (70.9 points) and Fast Express (67.3 points).[29] Among them, SF Express ranked first (see Table 4.1).

Brand	Duration of the whole transport journey	Processing time at departure	Duration of transportation	Processing time at the destination	Delivery time	Rate of punctuality
SF Express	1	1	2	1	1	1
EMS	2	2	1	2	8	2
Yunda Express	3	6	3	5	5	3
ZTO Express	4	4	4	7	4	4
YTO Express	5	3	6	6	7	5
STO Express	6	8	5	8	3	6
Best Express	7	5	7	4	9	7
ZJS Express	8	9	9	3	2	8
TTK Express	9	10	8	9	6	9
Fast Express	10	7	10	10	10	10

TABLE 4.1

PERFORMANCE AND RANKING OF THE TOP TEN DELIVERY SERVICE BRANDS IN 2017

Additionally, the State Post Bureau conducted a survey regarding satisfaction with express delivery services in 2017. The announcement stated:

> *As for reception, the average satisfaction scores of ordinary reception by phone call, unified customer service reception and online ordering were respectively 86.7, 82.8 and 83.9, which have improved in comparison with 2016. The service quality of these express enterprises concerning their ordinary reception by phone call is relatively high, and the scores do not differ much from each other. However, they vary greatly in unified customer service reception. Online reception as a new method has been accepted by users but still has room for improvement. Enterprises with good performance in reception procedures include SF Express, ZTO Express and Yunda Express. …*
>
> *As for delivery, the average satisfaction feedback score after acceptance was 79.6 points, 2.4 points higher than that in 2016. The scores for real-time notification, service quality, delivery scope notification and satisfaction about deliverers were respectively 78.2 points, 83.3 points, 79.0 points and 83.1 points. Enterprises with good performances are SF Express, ZTO Express and EMS.*
>
> *As for after service, the inquiry service had the best performance, with a satisfaction score of 86.5 points, rising 0.4 points in comparison with 2016; the satisfaction score of the complaint service was lower, 50.3 points, dropping 1.1 points in comparison with 2016. Enterprises with good after-service performance are SF Express, Yunda Express and ZTO Express.*[30]

This announcement was ample proof that SF Express was exceptionally prominent in its efficiency, with a performance that customers were quite satisfied with. Relatedly, SF Holding handed in a good financial report in 2017. According to its annual report for that year, it realized a revenue of ¥71.1 billion, an increase of 23.68%. The net profit attributable to the listed company was ¥4.8 billion, an increase by 14.12% year on year, as shown in Table 4.2.

	2017	2016	Comparison with Previous Year	2015
Revenue (¥)	71,094,296,984.46	57,482,698,073.15	23.68%	48,101,154,759.50
Net profit attributable to the shareholders of the listed company (¥)	4,770,689,703.15	4,180,426,152.00	14.12%	1,101,430,807.30
Net profit attributable to the shareholders of the listed company, with recurring profit and loss deducted (¥)	3,702,637,496.23	2,643,209,426.99	40.08%	753,509,926.89
Net cash flow from operating activities (¥)	6,108,333,011.73	5,675,037,785.87	7.64%	2,782,081,832.55
Basic earnings per share (¥/share)	1.12	1.06	5.66%	0.28
Diluted earnings per share (¥/share)	1.12	1.06	5.66%	0.28
Return on equity	18.43%	22.46%	-4.03%	7.83%

	At the end of 2017	At the end of 2016	Comparison with the End of the Previous Year	At the End of 2015
Total assets (¥)	57,660,164,354.37	44,134,885,588.74	30.65%	34,716,573,312.30
Net assets attributable to the shareholders of the listed company (¥)	32,680,826,795.10	20,511,767,66.96	59.33%	13,695,736,209.49

TABLE 4.2

OPERATING REVENUE OF SF HOLDING IN 2017

In the annual report, the proportion of income from new business was also disclosed. The report revealed that new business, including heavy freight, cold chain transportation, intra-city distribution and international business, had increased from 9.9% in 2016 to 13.5% in 2017.

Through the study of this financial report, it can be seen that although the income from new business had increased significantly, there was still great potential to be exploited, especially in the B2B sector. Hence, SF's aggressive approach was reasonable, for it was aiming to expand its B2B operations. This was also one of the key reasons why it spent ¥5.5 billion to acquire DPDHL's supply chain business in China, with an agreement reached between the companies on 26 October 2018.

Through this agreement, SF Hong Kong (a wholly owned subsidiary of SF Holding) would acquire in cash 100% of the shares from DHL Supply Chain (Hong Kong) Ltd, which were held by Deutsche Post Holding and Ocean Holding, and 100% from DHL Logistics (Beijing) Ltd, which were held by DHL Freight. DHL Beijing and DHL Hong Kong were the main bodies of DPDHL's supply chain business in mainland China, Hong Kong and Macao. After the completion of the ¥5.5 billion transaction, SF Hong Kong or its designated wholly owned subsidiary would become the sole shareholder of DHL Hong Kong and DHL Beijing.

The completion of this transaction signified SF Holding's further exploration and advancement in the field of B2B. Wang Xing, the founder of Meituan, said on the supply chain and B2B business:

> *Recently, my judgement is that if the next wave of the Chinese internet's recovery is to come, innovations in the fields of the supply chain and B2B industry will be an important driving force in that direction. So this is a matter of the supply side. [Regarding] past problems and possible solutions, if reform has to be enacted, what kinds of reforms could be applied to realize innovative ideas and change their efficiency costs?*

In the process of developing B2B, Wang Wei had his own considerations. In addition to the share of business volume, Wang not only paid attention to overall revenue but also to providing excellent services for middle and high-end customers.

In its strategic adjustment for the future, SF Express has been committed to providing integrated logistics services. While continuing to explore the ¥400 billion traditional express distribution market, it is always ready to sail into the blue ocean market of logistics. Especially during the present era of Internet+ (i.e. applications of the internet in conventional industries), by using big data analysis and cloud computing technologies to understand customers' needs, solve their difficulties and help them to develop, it has provided customers with many packaged solutions that include warehousing, sales forecasting, big data analysis, logistics and delivery, as well as financial management.

Having acquired the supply chain business of DHL, which was famous for its B2B operations, SF Express seemed to have been enormously strengthened. While upgrading its own industrial chains, the company's process of strategic transformation was also accelerated. This both demonstrated Wang's mindset of preparing for rainy days and underlined the strategic significance of B2B for SF Express.

ONE-STOP INTEGRATED LOGISTICS SOLUTIONS

As a rule in the business world, cooperation between the strong will only make them stronger. As a good practitioner of this rule, Wang Wei prefers to cooperate with more competitive players in the industry, such as UPS (United Parcel Service), HAVI Group and DHL.

Researchers have been optimistic about SF Express's acquisition of the supply chain business from DHL, even believing that it would lead to a restructuring of the competitive layout of the logistics industry in China. The reason for this high acclaim is that Wang's B2B strategy could provide continuous cash flow for SF Express in the future. In this regard, Wang claimed that, although SF Express did not have sufficient experience in the B2B field, it must not miss this opportunity and had to seize it immediately, because there had been signs of drastically changed needs among large numbers of customers. In order to better integrate the whole supply chain, SF Express once even considered outsourcing all of its logistics services to one specific logistics company. Therefore, this acquisition was in accordance with SF Express's underlying logic – to create one-stop integrated logistics solutions for customers.

Wang stated:

The organizational structures and business modes of today's four international express giants can be a reference for SF Express's mid-term and long-term development. The decentralized tender mode now prevalent in China – choosing a supplier for bulk logistics, another for express delivery, and then another for warehousing and e-commerce distribution – will probably change in the near future. Therefore, we must invest resources to do our best in the field right now.

In Wang's view, as the largest express and supply chain company in the world, DHL has many systemic and technological advantages for others to learn from, especially regarding its supply business.

According to DHL's official website in Chinese, the company has three core businesses: DHL Express, DHL Global Forwarding and DHL Supply Chain. With these three core services, DHL's business covers more than 100 countries and regions worldwide. As the world's largest contract logistics provider, DHL provides customized logistics solutions covering whole value chains for large enterprises from more than 50 countries and regions. Its official website states:

We have a wide range of solutions that can be tailored to your business' particular needs. Our aim is to optimize and improve your supply chain, helping you gain a competitive advantage.

Wang understood the competitiveness of DHL's supply chains, especially given that the maturity of its business had been proved by the stability of its sales volume in China. Data show that this part of DHL's business generated revenue of ¥3.5 billion in 2017. Wang's strategic goal was quite clear – to make SF Express a standard international integrated logistics solutions provider. According to SF Holding's annual report in 2017:

> *Now SF Holding Co Ltd is a leading integrated logistics service provider in China. After years of development, it has acquired the capability to provide integrated logistics solutions for customers. SF Express not only provides high-quality logistics services at the distribution end but also extends its services into production, supply, sales and distribution, which are at the front end of the value chain. By attending to customers' needs, the company uses big data analysis and cloud computing technology to offer an integrated logistics service covering warehousing management, sales forecasting, big data analysis and financial management. The company's logistics services mainly include various express services, such as time-definite express, economy express, inter-city distribution, warehousing services, international express and other types; freight services, such as standard logistics shipping, heavy freight shipping and other types; and cold chain transport services for customers in the fields of food and medicine. In addition, SF Holding provides value-added services such as price insurance and collection of payments to meet customers' individual needs.*
>
> *Over time, based on the diversified needs of different industries, customer groups and situations,*

> *SF Holding has upgraded product design and has shifted to the principle of 'providing user-centric and demand-oriented services.' The company focuses on the characteristics of the express industry, investigates customers' needs for end-to-end services in different situations, designs high-quality and differentiated products and services that are suitable for different customer groups, and reallocates internal resources and optimizes its products through product design.*[31]

Therefore, Wang has succeeded in providing customers with multi-categorical and all-round logistics services according to their needs, as shown in Figure 4.3.

EXPRESS DELIVERY

Intra-city	**China (INC.HMT)**	**International**	**Value-added services**		
SF Rush	SF Same Day Delivery SF Next Morning Delivery SF Standard Express SF Economy Express Logistics Cargo Service Heavy Freight Package Small-size LTL Heavy Freight FTL EC-Ship	SF Standard Express (International) SF Economy Express (International) SF E-Parcel International Heavy Freight SFBuy Direct Signature Service (DSS) SF Overseas Fulfillment/ Warehouse SF International	Common Shipment Protection Plus (SPP) Highly Secured Express Service Cash on Delivery (COD) Return Proof of Delivery Packaging Service Pickup Authorization Service Reverse Logistics Change of Address for Intra-city Delivery Change of Payment Mode	Formal Customs Declaration Electronic Acceptance Return Under Original Waybill Fixed Time Delivery Insurance Policy Delivery Special Warehousing Service To-door-Large-size-Shipment-Delivery	Overweight and Oversize Surcharge Holiday Service Door-to-door Delivery Residential Surcharge Fuel Surcharge SF Certified International Shipping (SF CIS) Shipment Storage Surcharge Remote Area Surcharge

COLD CHAIN		WAREHOUSING
Food Service	**Pharmaceutical**	**Warehousing**
Fresh Product Delivery Service Cold Chain Express Hairy Crab Special Delivery Cold Chain Economy Express Cold Chain To Store SF Cold Chain LTL Cold Chain LTL Cold Chain Warehousing	PharmaEase Pharmaceutical Special Delivery SF Pharmaceutical LTL Pharmaceutical LTL Pharmaceutical Warehousing	Standard Warehousing Management Core Competence

FIGURE 4.3

WEBSITE MENU DEPICTING SF EXPRESS PROVIDING CUSTOMERS WITH MULTI-CATEGORY AND ALL-ROUND LOGISTICS SERVICES ACCORDING TO THEIR NEEDS

It can be seen from the 2017 annual report how Wang has been planning and how he has succeeded in this field.

Wang's strategy is that any attempt at acquisition must obey the capital logic of 1 + 1 > 2. In May 2017, UPS announced that it would establish a joint venture with SF Holding in Hong Kong. Then, in August 2018, SF Holding established a joint venture with HAVI Group to form New HAVI. Finally, in October 2018, SF Holding bought DHL's supply chain business in China. Whether in the form of joint ventures or acquisitions, the purpose of SF Express is to cooperate with the frontrunners in various fields and ultimately, by combining their advantages, to effectively realize synergies between the market and technology. Meanwhile, through such investment, it can also obtain the rare resources required for its strategic growth.

In this way, the asset-heavy SF Holding, which was different from the asset-light DHL, would gain access to the latter's sophisticated management and technology for a modern enterprise. For DHL, the advantage was the ability to use the basic resources of SF Holding, such as land, warehouses and transport facilities, to reduce its costs.

Frank Appel, CEO of DPDHL, said:

> *The combination of our advantages will enable DPDHL Group and SF Holding to create a unique platform to meet the market need for a high-quality end-to-end supply chain provider in China. SF's local market expertise is an advantage for us to cater to our customers across a multitude of industries from technology, healthcare, retail and automotive to e-commerce. With DPDHL Group's global operating standards and all-covering network support, this will greatly facilitate our supply chain business and will provide a solid foundation for us to further explore and to find more opportunities in the Chinese market during the coming years.*

BE INNOVATIVE

Between the quality of its services, on the one hand, and its market share and business volume, on the other, Wang Wei clearly pays more attention to the former, especially to high-quality services for middle and high-end customers. Correspondingly, Wang has directed a series of reforms in SF Express. In 2014, in order to provide better-quality services, SF Express made a series of bold changes, such as proposing the 'Heike' business mode for serving customers offline (see below) and acquiring high-grade local distribution enterprises all over the country.

In the process of reform, Wang has never felt complacent and has rationally concluded that half of SF Express's innovations have been failures. He reflected on the reasons for such failures and managed to find solutions:

> *In 2014, SF has experienced the most innovations and changes in over 20 years. Many business departments have been established, and many new businesses have been created. At the same time, the total business volume has experienced explosive growth. Although there have been many innovations, in my opinion, almost half of them have been unsuccessful. The main reasons for our failures are inadequate preparations and planning, which are manifested in the following aspects.*
>
> *First, insufficient preparation in terms of the resource of talent. When entering a new field, we must be well prepared and have all kinds of talents. But we almost failed to do so.*
>
> *Second, there are variations when undertaking new businesses. We have indiscriminately applied the innovations to the whole of our network, letting each part undertake new business, so there was a dilemma – on the one hand, for the original members of staff, these new businesses were too difficult to handle and required too much change in themselves; on the other hand, too much attention has been paid to promoting new business, which has inevitably affected the quality of traditional business.*

In Wang's view, the focus of competition between enterprises currently is to improve operational efficiency and the strategy for new businesses. In order to enact a successful relocation, SF Express must pay particular attention to the trio of 'operation, capital and innovation.' In order to better work on these three aspects, SF Express should accelerate its processes of innovation and self-transformation through mergers, acquisitions and joint ventures.

As for the cooperation with DPDHL, Wang said:

> *SF has been actively improving its capabilities in the field of enterprise services for a long time, and is moving toward the goal of becoming the best integrated logistics solution provider in the eyes of customers. The cooperation with DPDHL Group will enhance the strength of SF's supply chain services in various industries. At the same time, it will enable us to transplant the leading management experience into the operation of supply chain business, and make us a supply chain solution service provider who knows more about customers. ... By working with DPDHL Group, a leading global company, this agreement will help us realize our vision of a global development.*

FORGING NEW CHAINS OF INDUSTRY

In several of his speeches to the company, Wang Wei has repeatedly stressed that "adventurous spirit," "innovative attitude" and "commitment" are essential qualities of an employee. These are advocated in SF Express's culture.

In Wang's view, "adventurous spirit" and "innovative attitude" are inseparable. Consistently, Wang has not only invested heavily in innovation but has also promoted innovation with the support of science and technology, so as to improve SF Express's service speed. Wang once said in an interview with CCTV-2:

In fact, I have been constantly emphasizing investment in science and technology. That means, I think, to rely on science and technology to re-evaluate all these resources, to manage them systematically, and then to regulate in the background with AI. Because in the future, AI and big data will reshape all walks of life, and will forge new chains to substitute the unfit ones. This process can be an opportunity for many enterprises, yet it will be a great risk for many others, who may die out in the process. So we have to look closely at the changes to industry that will be brought by future technologies.

If you can get connected with future technology, you will be able to catch the opportunity, otherwise you may be driven out. That is to say, you should focus on how to get connected with the internet, with high tech in this area. A stir of air can either indicate a breeze or foreshadow a tornado. I have constantly emphasized this point.

Therefore, according to our definition, our requirement of 'being fast' does not merely mean delivery speed. First, I don't think that's the correct definition. It should be the speed at which we respond to customers' needs. Second, the issue is whether we can keep up with the pace of technological development. I think this is the second most important meaning of 'speed.'

Without these two definitions, the so-called speed is of little value, as you know. Because if these two speeds are achieved, the speed of delivering will not be any problem. Either it will be easier to achieve, or we can say, we will better meet the needs of our customers: we can be fast or slow according to our customers' demands.

Wang knows that, to promote real speed, SF Express should not be too radical. This means he should not make large-scale and disruptive innovations, but enact change in a continuous way and in accordance with the actual situation of the company.

A large number of cases have proved that any large-scale disruptive innovation is unsuitable for giant enterprises, which should rather schedule change in a continuous way. Under this premise, if a giant enterprise like SF Express wants healthy and sustainable growth, it can only apply disruptive innovations on a small scale, in such a way as to serve its long-term prosperity.

In contrast to the giant companies, start-ups tend to be more radical in the process of innovation. In order to break the blockade set by mega-enterprises against competition, they often choose to adopt disruptive innovations to make themselves stand out.

So-called disruptive innovation is a concept that derives from a theory put forward by Clayton Christensen, the founder of Innosight and a professor of business management at Harvard Business School. According to Christensen, the theory aims to describe the impact of new technology (revolutionary change) on the survival and development of enterprises.

Christensen first proposed the term 'disruptive technologies' in 1997 in *The Innovator's Dilemma: When New Technologies Cause Great Firms to Fail*. In the book, Christensen states:

> *From recurrent facts we can see that the enterprises, which have perished as a consequence of the emergence of new consumer-supply paradigms, should have*

foreseen the significance of disruptive technologies, yet they remained indifferent until it was too late.[32]

Christensen's reasoning is that the leaders of these big companies only concentrate on what they think they should do, such as serving their most profitable customers and focusing on the most lucrative products with the most alluring profit margins. As such, they always choose to follow a path of mild and continuous innovation, which opens the door to their own destruction as a result of disruptive technologies. This tragedy occurs because the existing process of allocating the company's resources is always oriented toward sustainable innovations and maximization of profit. So the focus is mostly on existing customers and the proven market. However, once disruptive innovations occur – perhaps offering a cheaper and more convenient substitute for existing products, targeting low-end consumers or fostering a completely new consumer group – the existing companies immediately become paralysed.

Christensen suggests that entrepreneurs' response is often to turn to the high-end market rather than actively getting involved with these new technologies and sticking to the low-end market. But disruptive innovations will keep on growing and progressing, and will gradually erode the market share of traditional enterprises until they finally overcome the dominance of traditional products.

Based on this theory, any enterprise that seeks new business growth tends to achieve it through two forms of innovation. The first is sustaining innovation, through which they can seize the market out of the hands of market forerunners. The second is disruptive innovation, which enables them to open up a new market or take root among the lowest-end customer groups that consume their present products.

FAULT-TOLERANCE MECHANISMS IN INNOVATION

Express delivery is a traditional industry. And, as a leader in such an industry in the era of Internet+, what Wang Wei has been particularly concerned about is that his company must maintain a highly intensive degree of innovation, especially guarding against the impact of disruptive innovations. There are two reasons for this.

First, due to the trend of leading through technological innovation, no matter whether company managers believe it or not, their rivals are surely attaching more and more importance to technological innovation. As a result, these rivals' interest in innovation will strengthen their competitiveness. Yet for those who do not invest or invest very little in innovation, this situation is undoubtedly unfavourable.

Second, innovation concerning disruptive technologies will lower an industry's threshold. Some small cross-industry companies may carry their own disruptive technologies into the express industry, start from a particular market segment, and then quickly become a hidden champion in a certain region, thus threatening the survival of the entire industry.

For this reason, if SF Express wants to keep its competitiveness, it must have sufficient insight into current technological innovation trends. Wang believes that the most effective way to keep SF Express innovative is to meet customers' needs and establish a supportive management system.

When interviewed by the media, many managers of SF Express have said that their company has changed rapidly, both in its organizational structure and in its business. For example, one manager said: "It's mainly because there is a relatively well-functioning fault-tolerance mechanism. Wang Wei encourages innovations in any new business. And in the two most recent years, he has talked more about corporate transformation in company-wide speeches than before."

A review of SF Express's innovation history tells us that the company has always been trying to break through various business bottlenecks. In June 2012, the new brand SF Best was launched, with high hopes placed on it. This move indicated that Wang was beginning to tap into e-commerce, especially by focusing on the business of medium and high-end food, and the move drew wide attention from the media and scholars.

In 2013, supervised by Wang, SF Express made another move – it opened SF Heike stores in communities around the country. Several years before the initiative, SF had set up business divisions (e-commerce, supply chain and so on), and the company had been providing many integrated services, including express logistics, e-commerce logistics, auto-mobility logistics, food and medical services, financial and insurance services, and international e-commerce services. The purpose was to provide one-stop integrated logistics solutions for customers.

However, not all of these innovative efforts paid off, and some even became costly lessons. For example, SF Heike was created to deal with the 'sore point' of the last 100 metres at both ends of logistics (picking up and delivering). But, instead of solving this issue (often called the offline-to-online problem), the result was not satisfactory. After two years of endeavour, the stores had to change their name to SF Home in 2015. And later, in September 2016, SF Home was again changed to become part of the existing brand SF Best and merged with the online e-commerce business, so as to be included in SF Holding. The story reveals the little-known hardships experienced by Wang in his exploration of new business.

In an article titled "Innovation and Change: From 'SF Express' to 'SF Service,'" Wang wrote:

> *When I founded SF Express in Shunde in 1993, I was only 22 years old. I still remember the hard years when every day I had to commute between Shunde and Hong Kong by land, carrying a huge backpack full of contracts, letters, samples and customs declaration materials. At that time, I dared not expect that SF Express would grow up to its current scale, with annual sales over ¥20 billion and a valuation of ¥32 billion. Now it is a private enterprise that can compete with EMS of China Postal Express and Logistics.*
>
> *Although the company has undergone rapid development, I still have a sense of crisis if there is no innovation or change over three months. Many people ask, well, does an express company need that much innovation?*
>
> *In company-wide speeches, I have emphasized many times that the spirit of adventure, innovation and commitment must be advocated as the culture of SF Express. It has been 21 years since the company's establishment in 1993. SF Express has witnessed its own changes year by year. Here, what is never changeable is change itself. For example, we dared to break free from the franchise mode and promote regular chains. Another example is that we started to build our own freight airline in 2009 and became the first express company to transport parcels using its own aircraft in the same year.*

The year of 2013 is a year of change, both for me and for SF Express. This year, we have experimented with several important things that SF Express has never tried in the past 20 years, one of which is to promote strategic transformation.

On 19 August 2013, SF Express signed contracts with Oriza Holdings, China Merchants Group and CITIC Capital, agreeing that the total investment of the latter three would not exceed 25% of SF Express's shares, which totalled ¥8 billion. This was the first time in 20 years that SF Express had introduced outside investors. It allowed SF Express to gain stronger financial support for ongoing land purchases to expand its transit depots and the aviation hub, as well as for upgrading our automatic systems and automation equipment.

Today, SF Express has more than 200,000 employees. Without excellent managers, it would be impossible for me to direct the operation of all of our businesses. In order to enact transformation, the most critical thing is to make changes to employees' mentality and the whole corporate culture.

This shows that what Wang really cares about is competitiveness in the future. He believes that despite any number of challenges, SF Express should be able to return to the apex after every round of ups and downs.

The reform of SF Express advocated by Wang has been no less than an enlightenment to many Chinese entrepreneurs. In any era and in any industry, entrepreneurs must take the initiative to change, forget about their old advantages and break the old rules, so as to win in the oncoming competition.

CHAPTER 5

RENAMING SF HEAVY GOODS AND GOING PUBLIC

In our domestic express industry, we are constantly facing competition from the four international express giants. Once a company goes public, it will have to disclose its information and become almost transparent to investors. ... So, as a business owner, you have to know why you're going public. Otherwise, you will be caught in the dilemma described by the Buddhist saying, "If you act against the original mind and forget the existence of Truth, you will be entangled in puzzlement about Truth itself."

– Wang Wei

HEAVY FREIGHT EXPRESS, THE MOAT OF THE FORTRESS

Facing fierce competition in China's express delivery market, Wang Wei had to adjust his strategy, which was reflected in the renaming of SF Heavy Goods Group as SF Heavy Freight Express Group.

In August 2018, SF Express started this adjustment and made a series of organizational rearrangements. The seemingly minor change of name actually revealed Wang's recognition and affirmation of the role that heavy freight plays. Such focused attention illustrated the importance of the heavy freight business in Wang's mind.

FROM SF HEAVY GOODS TO SF HEAVY FREIGHT EXPRESS

According to an in-house announcement, SF Express issued a "Notice on Renaming the Heavy Goods Group and Its Structure Adjustment," officially changing the name of

SF Heavy Goods Group to SF Heavy Freight Express. The notice was as follows:

> *In order to adapt to the changes in the market and express industry, to meet the needs of strategic development for express business, to further integrate and optimize resources, and to enhance the brand value and market competitiveness of the express business, the company has decided to change the name of the Heavy Goods Group to Heavy Freight Express, and accordingly adjust the relevant organizational structure.*[33]

In order to better promote the competitiveness of the business group, SF Express also carried out a comprehensive and integrated strategic adjustment of SF Heavy Freight Express.

According to this notice, the objective of the change was to better meet market demands. At the same time, it had another impact by reorienting the company toward the heavy freight business. That is to say, the expectation was that the renaming would enhance the brand value and market competitiveness of the company's express business.

According to the company's official website, SF Heavy Freight Express is divided into two parts. The first part is the business in mainland China, whose services are as shown in Figure 5.1.

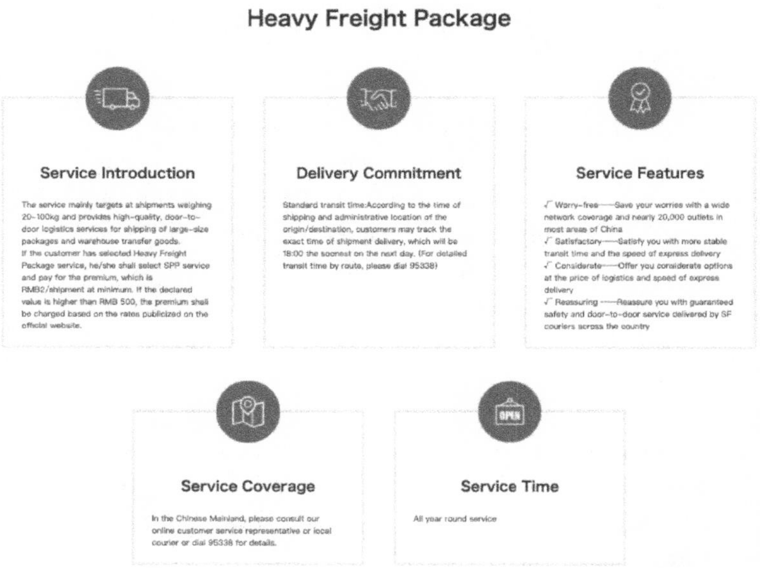

FIGURE 5.1

SF EXPRESS'S HEAVY FREIGHT EXPRESS SERVICES IN MAINLAND CHINA

The second part is the international heavy freight service, as shown in Figure 5.2.

FIGURE 5.2

SF EXPRESS'S INTERNATIONAL HEAVY FREIGHT SERVICE

Throughout the development of SF Express's heavy freight business since its initiation in 2014, its service products have gone through four stages (see Figure 5.3). First, in 2014, SF Express launched its Logistics Cargo Service. Second, from 2015 to 2016, SF Express successively launched its Heavy Goods FTL (full truck load) and Heavy Goods Express (air transportation) services. Third, in June 2017, SF Express launched dedicated ordinary transport services for the professional markets. Fourth, in January 2018, SF Express launched the 20–100 kg Heavy

Freight Package and the 100–500 kg Small-Size LTL (less than truck load) services.

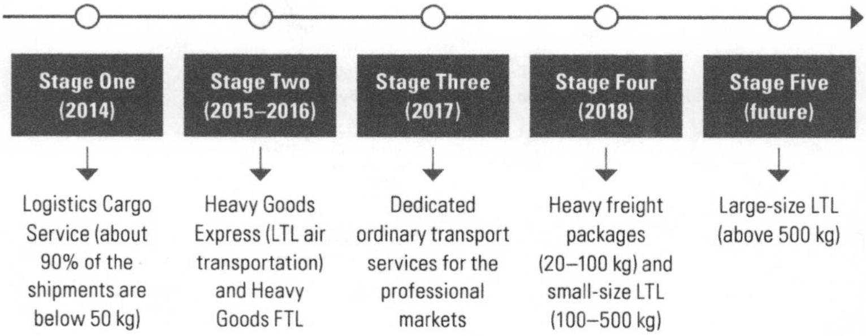

FIGURE 5.3
THE FOUR STAGES OF SF EXPRESS'S HEAVY FREIGHT BUSINESS

From the evolution of SF Heavy Freight Express, we can see that the first three stages cannot be regarded as those of a real express business. The reason is that the logistics cargo service of SF Heavy Goods had been operating within a lower weight range of kilograms for a long time.

Looking back at SF Express's development of its heavy freight business, it is not difficult to see that the company began to strengthen this sector in the second stage. The introduction of two modes of transportation (FTL and air transportation) was not merely an extension of the existing services with a higher weight range. In the third stage, SF Express began to expand its dedicated ordinary transport services. The key advantage was that the dedicated services facilitated direct transportation between professional markets. However, goods above 100 kg only accounted for about 10% of everything that was transported.

Therefore, SF Heavy Goods was at best dealing with large packaged products in the early two stages.

This situation did not change until the end of 2017. It is known that, by the end of 2017, only 25% of the goods accepted for carriage by SF Heavy Goods were above 100 kg.

Compared with Ane Express and Best Express, of whose goods 70% to 80% are above 100 kg, SF Heavy Goods was still lagging far behind. Data show that before 2018, when comparing their accepted goods above 100 kg, there was a huge gap between SF Express's logistics cargo service and its dedicated ordinary transport services, and those of the traditional LTL companies (see Figure 5.4).

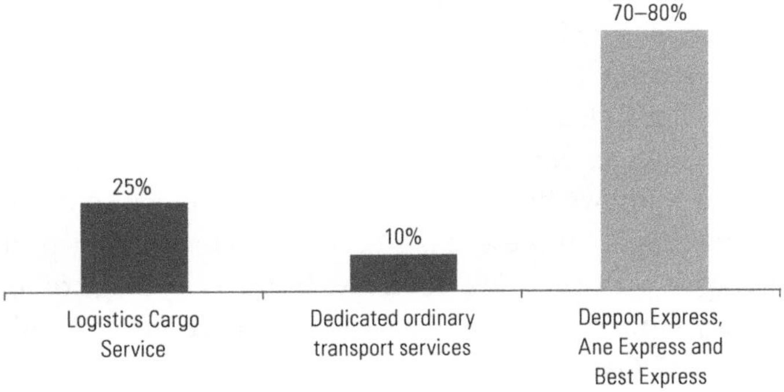

FIGURE 5.4

PERCENTAGE OF TRANSPORTED GOODS ABOVE 100 KG

1. Source: https://www.iyiou.com

Having completed these four stages, SF Express introduced a new service – 100–500 kg small-size LTL – breaking the ceiling of 100 kg. With this, it entered the realm of heavy goods express transportation.

With this mending of shortcomings, SF Express started to greatly improve its heavy freight business in two ways.

First, it improved its operative capability. Before this reconstruction, owing to an inadequate operative capability and a relatively high damage rate, it was natural that SF Express could not effectively meet the strict requirements for delivering large cargos. Previously, for a long time, in order to provide customers with excellent service, SF Express had not extended the kilogram weight range it handled. Although small-size LTL had been launched, it still needed to solve the problem of handling large cargos.

In order to solve this problem, SF Express cooperated with Xinbang Logistics, a traditional LTL enterprise, which had a unique capacity to cope with large cargos. In April 2018, the two companies set up Shunxin to undertake small-size LTL and loads above 100 kg via a logistics cargo service. Subsequently, Xinbang began to undertake small-size LTL and logistics cargo services for SF Express.

Second, SF Express improved its network coverage. As is widely known, for any express enterprise involved in the heavy freight business, it is a necessity to have a transport network with extensive coverage. In the early stage of SF Heavy Goods, its operative network was connected with that of SF Overnight Delivery.

After several years of development, there was no doubt that SF Express's heavy freight business required more depots and sites. In order to avoid being trapped in such bottlenecks, SF Express began to operate these businesses with separate networks.

By June 2018, SF Express had a total of 899 heavy freight service depots, mainly in East, South and Southwest China. Of course, there was still a great disparity, in the sense of depot numbers, between SF Express and such companies as Ane Express, Best Express, Deppon Express,

Yunda Express and ZTO Express. Figure 5.5 compares the networks of the main express enterprises in 2017.

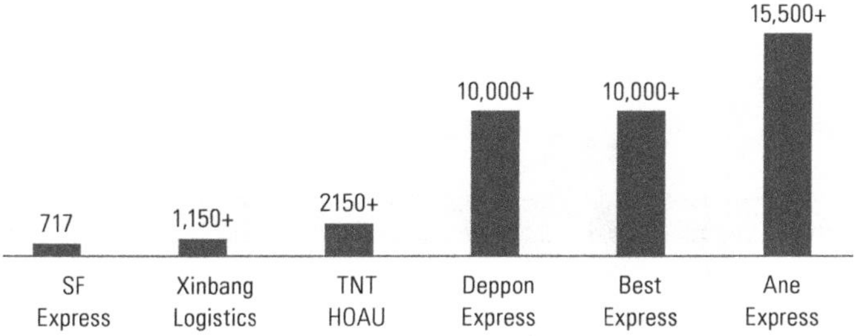

FIGURE 5.5

SERVICE DEPOT NUMBERS OF THE MAIN EXPRESS ENTERPRISES IN 2017

1. Source: https://www.iyiou.com

SF Express's alliance with Xinbang Logistics – to form Shunxin – was intended to combat this disparity and enable SF Express to catch up with its competitors. Xinbang already had more than 1,150 service depots, mainly distributed across East and South China.

The establishment of Shunxin undoubtedly increased the density of depot distribution for SF Express's heavy freight business in East and South China. Moreover, with the development of Shunxin, the number of depots would undoubtedly witness a continuous increase. Shunxin planned to set up over 10,000 depots by 2020, as shown in Figure 5.6.

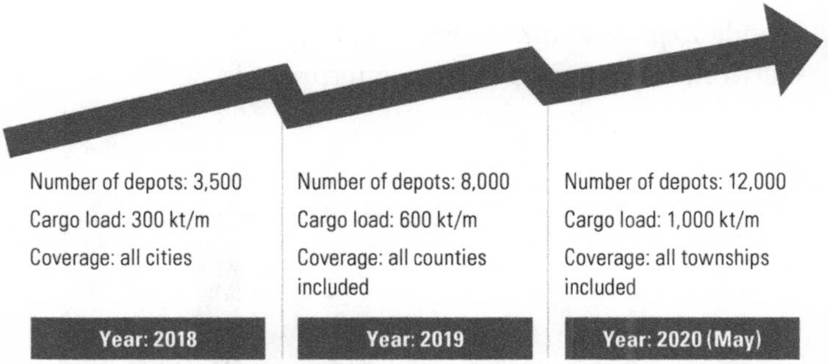

FIGURE 5.6
SHUNXIN'S THREE-YEAR PLAN FOR ITS NETWORK, 2018–2020 (KT/M: KILO-TONS PER MONTH)

1. Source: https://www.iyiou.com

For SF Express, the increase in the number of service depots was also a key to activating its retailing business (see Chapter 6), and it aimed to eventually operate in a mode akin to 'regular chains + franchises.' Data show that the number of SF Express's regular chain depots and Shunxin's franchised depots amounted to nearly 2,300 (over 1,300 belonging to Shunxin at present), which exceeded the number of TNT HOAU.

INCREASED CONTRIBUTION OF THE HEAVY FREIGHT BUSINESS

In the first half of 2018, the heavy freight business accounted for 8.1% of the total revenue of SF Group, and this sector had become one of the main forces behind SF Express's growth (see Figure 5.7). This growth was the determining factor behind the renaming of SF Heavy Goods as SF Heavy Freight Express and the adjustment to the organizational structure of the company. Also, it marked the real entrance of SF Express into the heavy freight express market.

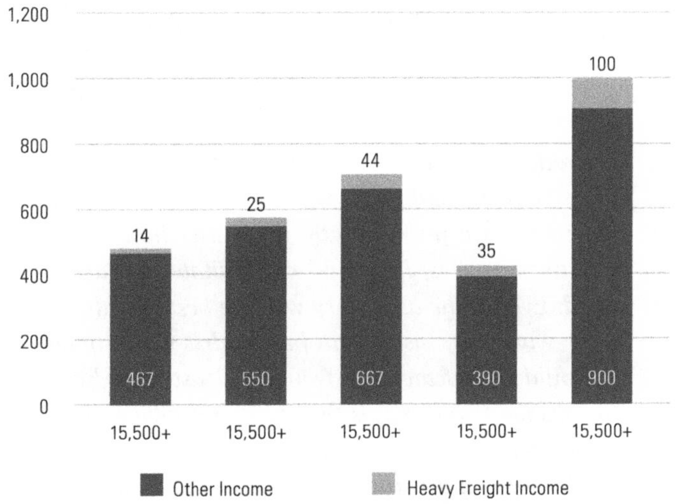

FIGURE 5.7
CHANGES IN SF EXPRESS'S GROSS INCOME AND HEAVY FREIGHT EXPRESS INCOME (¥)

As a latecomer, given its lack of experience in network design, distribution, equipment investment and especially the handling of large cargos, SF Express still had a long way to go to catch up with Deppon Express in the field of LTL.

Certainly, any enterprise that has taken a new strategic path must be decisive and resolute instead of swaying back and forth. If it is not, it will lose the best chance. After all, opportunity seldom knocks twice. What's more, Yunda Ground and ZTO Freight were also growing rapidly with their advantage of price, and this required Wang Wei to burn his boats to take advantage of the new opportunity. The situation for SF's heavy freight business at that moment meant it was better to embrace changes than act passively.

It was just like the spirit exhibited in the popular Chinese TV series named *Drawing Sword*. The hero, Li Yunlong, a regiment commander, shouts to mobilize his soldiers:

> *Comrades, let me first explain what the act of 'drawing sword' is. In ancient times, when a swordsman met his adversary on a narrow path, no matter how mighty his adversary was, he would not hesitate to draw his sword. Even if the adversary was the best swordsman in the world, against whom he couldn't win! Though he would be defeated, he would at least have had a glorious fight, and that is the 'spirit of drawing sword.' Every army has its own traditions. What is tradition? Tradition is what is rooted in our character and temperament. Even if we are vastly outnumbered, even if we are encircled, we are brave enough to draw our swords and fight to the last man! In a word, in a deadly fight, the braver man wins! The spirit of drawing sword is our soul! Draw your swords! We are invincible!*[34]

Under Wang's leadership, SF Express saw great achievements in 2018. The financial report showed that in the first half of that year, SF Holding had achieved a revenue of ¥42.5 billion, up 32.1% year on year, and achieved 60% of its annual target. The net income for shareholders reached ¥2.2 billion, up 18.6% year on year. The number of delivery packages reached almost 1.9 billion, up 35.3% year on year.

According to the data, the main business of SF Express was now divided into two parts: the traditional sector (time-definite and economy products) and the new sector (heavy freight, refrigerated transportation, intra-city express and international express).

In the traditional sector, time-definite products represent the competitiveness of SF Express and have always been an important contribution to the company's revenue, accounting for over 60% of the total. In the first half of 2018, the revenue of the company's traditional businesses had a growth rate of 18.2%. Moreover, after the company's integration of relatively similar products and optimization of the operative process, the revenue growth rate reached 53.7%.

This round of transformation showed significant effects. The half-year financial report of SF Express in 2018 showed that the company's new business had grown rapidly, with an overall income increase to 16.2% from 12.3% in the same period of 2017. Among this, the intra-city express business had a year-on-year increase of 158.8%, heavy freight saw growth of 95.8%, refrigerated transportation 47.7% and international express 40.8%.[35]

Meanwhile, SF Express kept on expanding into the area of new businesses. For example, it arrived at a strategic cooperation with Luckin Coffee, a popular brand, to deliver its takeaways. In the refrigerated transportation business, SF Express started a strategic cooperation with HAVI Group by establishing a joint venture, New HAVI, in August 2018. To develop the international market, SF Express invested in the American logistics service platform Flexport in April 2018.

It is worth noting that, in the sector of new businesses, Wang paid special attention to heavy freight. In the first eight months of 2018, the revenue from this business exceeded ¥4.4 billion, which had been the company's revenue for this sector in the whole of 2017.

GOING PUBLIC

Undeniably, one important reason for SF Express to go public was financing. In contrast to STO Express, YTO Express, Yunda Express and ZTO Express, SF Express has for a long time been a loyal practitioner of the regular chain mode (as opposed to franchises), so its debt-to-asset ratio is higher than the average level for the industry. According to data provided by Wind Financial Terminal, by 31 December 2015, the average debt-to-asset ratio in the Chinese express industry was 58.6%, while the debt-to-asset ratio of SF Express was 60.3%.

The reason for SF Express's high debt-to-asset ratio was that it had been investing heavily in its business expansion, including the construction of a transit airport, purchases of aviation equipment, refrigerated trucks and temperature-control equipment, and IT infrastructure. The huge amount of investment, especially on aviation, warehousing and cold chains, had undoubtedly put great pressure on the cash flow of SF Express. It would be difficult for the company to maintain such a high input of capital by merely relying on its own funds and bank loans.

Therefore, the company was in need of other funding sources. Going public was a decisive move that Wang Wei had to take. According to a report in 2015, by the end of the year, SF Holding had in hand monetary capital of ¥3.6 billion, ¥6.7 billion in the form of wealth management products and ¥14.2 billion available for payments in the short term. In terms of liabilities, the company had short-term loans that amounted to ¥6.6 billion, notes payable that amounted to ¥190.0 million, accounts payable that amounted to ¥3.1 million, payroll payable that amounted to ¥2.7 billion, taxes payable that amounted to ¥575.0 million, interest payable that amounted to ¥14.8 million and non-current liabilities due within one year that amounted to ¥673.0 million. All its short-term payment debts totalled ¥13.8 billion.

THE BRIGHT SIDE OF LISTING

Wang Wei, who had persistently refused outside investors, now had to embrace the capital market, because of the company's adoption of a new operating mode and the successive listing of its rivals. The need was so urgent that in February 2017 he finally chose back-door listing through Dingtai New Material instead of an initial public offering (IPO).

One of the benefits of Wang's entry into the capital market was obvious. In only six days, his personal wealth was boosted from ¥13 billion to ¥180 billion, ranking third in China. His wealth surpassed Tencent founder Ma Huateng's ¥167 billion and sat behind that of only Wang Jianlin, the founder of Wanda Group, and Jack Ma, the founder of Alibaba Group.

It was almost unbelievable that, a month earlier, Wang had been an inconspicuous entrepreneur. Keeping a low profile, he had scarcely accepted any interviews and left no traces of himself in newspapers or on TV. His name could not even be found on the China Rich List 2016. However, the necessity of a capital infusion finally urged him to allow SF Express to go public. In 2017, Wang was ranked fourth on the China Rich List. After the listing, Wang and SF Express soon became the frequent subjects of major media headlines.

Data shows that, in the six days after its listing, the shares of SF Express hit the limit six times in succession, reaching a market value of ¥280 billion and ranking 15th on the Shanghai Stock Exchange and the Shenzhen Stock Exchange.

This phenomenon made entrepreneurs in traditional businesses in China feel happy but also distressed. They were happy to witness an era when a company's share value could miraculously increase by over 66% in only six days in the magical A-share market. But they were distressed because they regretted not having entered the capital market earlier and realized they had lost a chance to be accredited by the media and the capital market for their financing and managerial performance.

SF Express had an obvious fundamental advantage over other private express companies in the A-share market. According to a business report released on 22 February 2017, SF Holding yielded a net profit of ¥4.18 billion in 2016, which was 1.92 times its previously set target. This excellent performance brought much confidence to the capital market. However, the high price-to-earnings (P/E) ratio of SF Holding was to become the main cause for the following decline of the company's stock value. The P/E ratio of SF Holding in 2016 was 90.9, which was 1.73 times that of YTO Express, 2.1 times that of Yunda Express, 2.45 times that of STO Express and 2.47 times that of ZTO Express. In addition, the P/E ratio of SF Holding was significantly higher than the average of Shenzhen Stock Exchange, which was 30.4 by 27 February 2017.[36]

AGAINST MERGERS AND ACQUISITIONS

For any developing enterprise, mergers and acquisitions is a topic that cannot be easily bypassed. Generally, when the scale of a company reaches a certain degree, it will either acquire or be acquired by others.

This was exactly the situation when SF Express achieved a certain scale. At the time, after the listing,

FedEx, UPS and other overseas giants repeatedly offered olive branches. Knowing these multinational companies' intention was nothing but mergers and acquisitions, Wang repeatedly refused.

In the golden times of the express industry, some companies were so eager to earn quick money that they turned to other businesses. In contrast, Wang refused these temptations and aimed at improving SF Express's professional and standardized management, the company's efficiency, and customers' experience.

This is why Liu Miao, the former president of SF Best, once told the media that Wang was the richest workaholic he had ever met. The fundamental reason for such diligence is that Wang was both a boss and a courier in his early days, and he still keeps a sense of this dual role. For more than 20 years, Wang has been working more than 14 hours each day, and even regularly goes to the front line of working sites to send and receive packages for customers.

This is inseparable for Wang's sense of crisis.

As an executive of SF Express, Xu Yong believes that Wang's most valuable traits include his insistence on professionalization and his invulnerability to interesting temptations. The strategy of professionalization undoubtedly improved the core competitiveness of SF Express in its initial stage of capital accumulation, which enabled it to concentrate its limited capital and talent resources on the process of information construction and standardization, thus ensuring it would become a hidden champion.

In spite of his bold manoeuvres in corporate management, Wang remains unusually low-key and still rarely accepts interviews with the media. Even the company's in-house magazine, *Communication*, has never published a photo or any exclusive interview.

On the other hand, Wang pays considerable attention to the personal development of his employees. Even during the most difficult times of financial crisis, he did not lay off one single employee.

Wang often says things like "couriers are the nicest people in SF Express," both in his in-company speeches and in public meetings. It is true that Wang has paid unprecedented attention to his employees. His refusal of mergers and acquisitions may partly be out of concern that the subsequent management adjustment and change to the corporate culture would be detrimental to the interests of these people.

LISTING AS A WAY TO SOLVE THE PROBLEM OF A MONEY SHORTAGE

SF Express was officially listed on 24 February 2017, although Wang was not very enthusiastic about it. He once commented:

> *Listing is nothing more than obtaining the capital needed for the company's development. SF Express is short of money, but it cannot go public for money itself. After going public, the company will become a money-making machine. Every change in the stock price agitates the company, which is very harmful to the management of the company.*

Because of this belief, for a long time Wang had resisted such topics as exterior capital injection or listing. There even circulated various stories about Wang's rejection of investors. For example, in 2004, FedEx intended to expand into the Chinese market and planned to buy SF Express at the price of ¥5 billion. Facing this lucrative offer, Wang resolutely refused, despite the fact that in the same year, the whole volume of SF Express's sales was just ¥1.3 billion.

But venture investors would not ignore such a potential champion. One by one they expressed their willingness to invest in this leading enterprise in the express delivery industry. One of them even spent ¥500,000 on intermediary fees, just to invite Wang to have a meal and a chat. In the face of this allurement, Wang did not agree.

A chairman of a consulting company once disclosed privately that many American investors, including Citibank, had asked him to persuade Wang to agree to an investment. Once the investment contract was successfully arranged, the chairman would receive a commission of US$10 million.

From his initial resistance to his acceptance of the need for listing, Wang must have experienced a painful inner struggle – especially after seeing the successive listings of STO Express, YTO Express and Yunda Express, which invigorated their respective teams through the new financing. In addition, after more than 20 years of maturation, the express industry had now reached the tip of the curve and was showing a downward tendency. All these factors determined that the once arrogant SF Express had no alternative but to show respect to the law of the capital market.

In order to quickly raise the needed funds, SF Express skipped the procedure of an IPO and opted for back-door listing. There were three reasons for this decision.

First, as SF Express was keen on developing multiple business groups at the time, the problem of the huge lack of operating funds needed to be solved urgently. As outlined in Chapter 4 and earlier in this chapter, the business scope of SF Express used to be focused on four aspects: express transportation, logistics, warehouse distribution and commerce, thus creating a mature supply chain system. However, in the following reorganization, the original division of business sectors was changed into an express transport business group, a commercial business group (Heike and SF Best), a supply chain business group (ordinary cargo service and cold chain), a warehouse distribution logistics business group (e-commerce and cross-border online shopping) and a financial services business group (SF Pay). All these businesses covered express delivery, fresh food e-commerce, cross-border e-commerce, financial payments and so on.

The purpose of this adjustment was not difficult to understand: the evolution within SF Express required more funds and resources, both to enhance the company's competitiveness and to extend the boundaries of its business.

Second, SF Express's rejection of the franchise mode, and its reliance on its own funds, had undoubtedly put unprecedented pressure on its development.

Looking back on the evolution of the whole express delivery industry, STO Express, YTO Express, Yunda Express and ZTO Express were gaining large shares of the market by fighting a price war on the foundation of their uses of the franchise mode. In addition, after each was listed, they also began to make their own strategic arrangements. Given that these competitors were successively making gains in the capital market using the franchise mode, they were a real threat to Wang.

To deal with the competition, which was becoming more and more fierce, SF Express had nothing to rely on but its own capital distribution.

Third, financing through listing could alleviate SF Express's high asset–liability ratio. The asset-liability ratio of SF Express remained around 50% (as of the end of 2012). Compared with international logistics giants, this number was better than that of UPS and similar to those of FedEx and EMS. Additionally, SF Express's liquidity ratio and quick ratio were even superior to those of EMS. However, one problem that could not be ignored was that SF Express's asset-heavy mode needed to be based on sufficient funds to ensure steady development.

LISTING OR NOT? TWO REASONS ARE ENOUGH

In the business circle of China, there used to be four entrepreneurs who were famous for not going public: Ren Zhengfei, Tao Huabi, Zong Qinghou and Wang Wei. Now Wang has left this idiosyncratic club.

Zong Qinghou, the founder of Wahaha, who had previously claimed that "we don't lack money and we won't go public," began to change his previous attitude, saying that he would consider going public at an appropriate time. Suddenly, there were media reports that Wahaha was ready to go public.

Rumours continued to spread about Wahaha and the other three members of the 'Non-listing Club,' suggesting that they would make the decision to go public. On 25 July 2018, Wang Hong, the deputy general manager of Shenzhen Stock Exchange, joined up with Guizhou Securities

Regulatory Bureau and Guizhou Provincial Finance Office, and went to Guizhou for a research tour of Guizhou Freight Car Band Technology Co Ltd, Guiyang Nanming Laoganma Flavor Food Co Ltd and Guizhou Yishu Chain Pharmaceutical Co Ltd. Since this visit was understood by many to include training programmes for the three companies, people naturally believed that these companies were preparing for listing. From that point, rumours that Laoganma (founded by Tao Huabi) would go public spread widely over the market. On 8 August 2018, Liu Tao, Tao Huabi's secretary, responded that "Shenzhen Stock Exchange just paid a visit. Laoganma will not go public, and there is no plan to go public in the future."

Usually, everything goes back to normal when a rumour is dispelled. However, the investment institutions would not let go of such an opportunity for hefty profits, which they felt were within the reach of their fingertips. Once again they spread the news that Laoganma would go public, which drew the public's attention another time. Having no choice, on 12 November 2018, Tao Huabi herself dismissed the rumour in an interview on Guizhou Radio TV Station: "Loans, equity participation, fundraising and listing are not in our plan. We develop as much as our own money can support."

Objectively speaking, in this gilded age, going public had already become a means for many enterprises to amass money. However, Laoganma's insistence on developing with its own money was undoubtedly a wisp of fresh air in the business world.

In an interview, Tao told the media her reason for not listing:

> *I told my son to be a good person and do business step by step. I asked him to promise that he would never buy any shares, never sell shares, never go public and never apply for loans. The four principles should be held by my children and grandchildren. If any government official talked to me about listing, I would tell him: "Don't even talk about it! No way! I won't squander my money, I swear on my life."*

Tao is very cautious about listing. She has always adhered to the policy of "no loans, no financing, no listing." Just as she said, even if the government tries to persuade her, she still dares to refuse.

For any enterprise, there are normally two reasons to go public: first, internal reasons, such as ownership structure, sufficiency of funds to expand the business and social demands; and second, external reasons, such as participating in projects advocated by government officials or adjusting to other market factors in mainland China.

Ren Zhengfei (the founder of Huawei) and Tao Huabi have been much admired by the business community in mainland China since 2014, because the two successful entrepreneurs both adhere to a common principle of not going public. Although they share the same idea, their reasons are the opposite. Tao once said: "I am determined not to go public. Once you go public, you may go broke. Going public means swindling people out of their money. People invest, and when the time comes, the market will suck their money away. Then it will be my responsibility to pay off their debts. I won't buy it." There have been many lengthy reports about Tao's determination and her belief that going public is like fraud, and these have made her the target of varying comments.

Tao Huabi founded Guiyang Nanming Laoganma Flavor Food Co Ltd in 1996. Over nearly 20 years of development, this enterprise transformed a common brand of cheap pepper sauce into an internationally famous one on US luxury retail websites. Tao has also become the icon of the largest pepper sauce enterprise in China.

Data show that in 2017, according to China National Radio, the annual revenue of Laoganma was ¥4.6 billion and its annual tax reached ¥755 million, ranking second among the top 100 private enterprises in Guizhou, after the ¥834 million paid by a local real estate developer.

In February 2018, Tao's secretary revealed at a media conference that:

> *In the past five years, the total sales revenue of our company has exceeded ¥20 billion, and the taxes paid have reached ¥3.2 billion. At present, the company's daily production capacity in making pepper products has exceeded 3 million bottles, with 24 series of products.*

Ren believes that the employees of Huawei are also owners of the company. They tend to take a long-term view and therefore are not eager to leave.

Ren once told *The Wall Street Journal*:

> *First of all, I don't know if the proposal from Poland will work or not. Poland is a small country, so it may not have such a big influence on the market. Germany and France may be more influential, by the way.*

> *Whether Polish companies can make a difference, I don't know yet. Even if Poland could achieve its goal, it would not be so vital for us. Because Huawei is not a listed company, and we don't need any attractive financial statement. If we lose markets in these countries, we would tune down our expectation accordingly. As long as we can support our employees, we have a future.*

There were various internal reasons for Huawei's not going public. Owing to the large number of original owners, Huawei's ownership structure was not very concentrated. Going public obviously meant that the management could lose control over the company. Even though the possibility was only faint, such things could happen and had been happening. Also, once Huawei became a listed company, many employees (as internal shareholders) would become millionaires and could lose their passion for working.

There is no denying that the most important reason for Laoganma and Huawei not to go public was that they had abundant liquid capital. When a company does not lack money for expansion or routine operations, it has no incentive to go public. This is because, once a company goes public, its strategic decisions and investment initiatives, as well as a lot of internal information, must be made public and monitored by shareholders and the media. Such information transparency is undoubtedly not very enticing for a private enterprise that has emerged from obscurity.

When entrepreneurs were lining up to list their enterprises in order to gain money, Tao Huabi refused to do so.

Her so-called eccentric behaviour not only enabled Laoganma to survive financial crisis but also led to the company outshining those that listed their companies after forging financial reports and those who were desperate to cash out when their business performance plummeted.

Some media reports suggested that Laoganma refused to go public because of Tao's own experience and her business perspective. That is, her mindset was to feel content with a small fortune. Yet they saw in SF Express a more attractive objective for investment capital. This was especially the case given that SF Express had more specialized business divisions and, in its aim of constructing a complete ecosystem, would need huge amounts of funds. Therefore, going public became the natural choice for SF Express.

Wang Wei was very clear that SF Express's going public was intended to accrue money for its future development. Indeed, he had said earlier: "The benefit of going public is nothing more than gaining the money needed to develop the company."

Data show that by 31 December 2015, SF Holding had a total of ¥14.2 billion available for payments in the short term and needed to pay only slightly less than ¥14.1 billion over the same period. The liquid capital of SF Holding was then only ¥360 million. This was obviously insufficient when compared with the company's scale and sales volume.

Data also show that the debt ratio of SF Holding was 33.4% in 2013, 47.34% in 2014 and 60.3% in 2015. In comparison, other express enterprises had not witnessed such a drastic rise. YTO Express even saw a decline in its debt ratio in 2015. After careful consideration,

Wang finally chose to allow SF Express to go public, because at the time he had no other choice in the face of his rivals. Insiders admitted in an interview: "In an era when capital is king, the choice of back-door listing is definitely best for financing. They who first seize the benefits brought by listing will have an opportunity to beat their rivals."

CHAPTER 6

COMMITTING TO RETAIL AND BUILDING A BUSINESS ECOSYSTEM

In the future, we will participate and be deeply involved in various industries instead of being limited to 'last mile logistics,' for the latter will never make us deep-rooted in any industry.

– Wang Wei

COMMITTING TO RETAIL

Wang Wei has concentrated on the strategic layout of retailing for more than ten years. For example, in SF Express's offline retail sector, both Heike and SF Home ended in failure, and most of the stores under the two brands were transformed into SF Best stores, in the mode of express delivery and convenience stores.

In regard to the current e-commerce boom, Wang is not willing to be left behind and is thus actively taking part in it. Although SF E-business Circle, a previous e-commerce platform, has been closed, and the only survivors are SF Best (an e-commerce platform for fresh commodities) and SF Overseas Online Shopping (a cross-border e-commerce platform), whose business achievements are not very remarkable, SF Express keeps on trying to be more involved in the retail sector.

SF EXPRESS'S ATTEMPT ON RETAIL

On 13 October 2016, Jack Ma, founder of Alibaba, put forward the concept of 'new retail' for the first time at the Apsara Conference. Ma said:

In the next 10 or 20 years, there will be no e-commerce. Only the concept of new retail businesses will survive.

That is to say, online and offline logistics must be combined to create a new form of retail business. Offline businesses must go online, and online businesses must go offline. Such a new retail model can only be achieved by combining online and offline retail with modern logistics.

In Ma's view, against the backdrop of upgraded consumerism, new technologies (which consist of AI, big data and cloud computing) are intended to enable a link between online and offline businesses, efficient logistics and innovations of the whole retail industry chain, thus naturally leading to 'new retail.' The emergence of new retail is certainly beneficial to consumers, and is more so to businesses and the real economy as a whole. The reason is that new retail may affect the business pattern in the next 10 or even 20 years. Wang Wei, who has been undertaking initiatives in the retail sector, thus naturally understands its commercial potential.

Based on this, Wang has set up a layout to develop in the retail sector, and this layout can be traced back to about 10 years ago. During the Dragon Boat Festival in 2009, a courier working at an SF district in Jiaxing City, Zhejiang Province, successfully sent out more than 1 million *zongzi* (a traditional Chinese type of glutinous rice dumpling) made by Wufangzhai. This seemingly accidental success consequently gave Wang a lot of confidence in getting onto the e-commerce platform.

In 2010, Wang officially launched SF E-business Circle, SF Express's e-commerce platform, which was mainly established to sell food products, and it also launched a payment platform, SF Treasure. However, what Wang then experienced can be described by two famous lines from a traditional Chinese poem: "I used to crave the bright moon, but the moon shines solely downward on the ditch."

Due to setbacks in the fields of e-commerce and payment, SF Express later embarked on another painful transformation. In 2012, Wang adjusted SF Express's business direction, seeing cold chain technology as a breakthrough and even treating it as the company's core competitive edge. The company set up SF Best, a fresh food e-commerce platform, which required high technology in terms of cold chain transport.

Wang had attached so much importance to this new project that, before the launch of SF Best, he flew from Shenzhen to Beijing to discuss the significance of this strategic move with some senior executives. He repeatedly stressed that "SF Best is a project that must succeed."

Under his supervision, SF Best gained a good record. On Double-11 Day (11 November) 2014, the sales volume of SF Best reached ¥70 million in a single day. Unfortunately, though, the platform still failed to attain high-frequency consumption.

Subsequently, SF Express began to seek a breakthrough in offline retailing. On 18 May 2014, it began to develop offline retail sales, launching Heike, a brand of community stores with network services. The business of Heike covered four major directions: commodity ordering, offline experiencing before online shopping, convenience service and express self-service.

Of course, Wang's decision to set foot in offline retail, which was especially exemplified by the Heike online community stores, aimed to solve the problem of the 'last mile' in logistics and also to seize the blue ocean market of residential communities. Shortly afterwards, Heike expanded into a network of more than 2,000 stores. During this rapid expansion, some problems were exposed. Despite officially being a retail brand, Heike was functioning more like a chain of express delivery stores where customers could collect express goods. The goods in the stores were only provided for display. When customers wanted to buy goods, they still had to place an order online. Therefore, the brand was criticized by customers, researchers and the media.

Yang Daqing, a contract research fellow at the China Logistics Association, said:

> *The main reason for the failure is that the company tried to do business based on a mode of thinking grounded in express delivery. ... SF Express does not understand the community economy. The biggest advantage of the community economy lies in convenience, fast speed and satisfactory experience, all of which are lacking in Heike.*

He Wen, a partner at Chunxiao Capital, shared similar views when he said: "For offline stores, the most important thing is 'to experience.' Given that there is no real commodity to be purchased and no services to be experienced, this shop does not conform to the rules of community retailing."

In He's opinion, the approach of Heike went completely against the essence of community retailing, namely efficiency, experience and cost control. Because of this, in 2015, SF Express had to close most of its Heike stores, and the remaining stores had to be renamed as SF Home.

In the same year, SF Express had started the process of listing, so it needed to strip away its commercial sector, which was responsible for online and offline retail business.

In 2017, SF Express was listed through the back door of Dingtai New Material. It disclosed relevant financial data showing that SF had lost ¥126 million, ¥614 million and ¥866 million in the 2013, 2014 and 2015, respectively, in the "stripped sector of commerce," with a combined loss of ¥1.6 billion. The reason for the loss, the report said, was "mainly due to SF Commercial's concentration on developing offline stores since 2014."[37]

A HARD FIGHT FOR THE 'LAST MILE'

Although SF had encountered a series of failed attempts in terms of its retailing strategy, Wang Wei did not give up hope about the retail business.

In order to revitalize SF Express's retailing business, Wang began to serve as the CEO of SF Commercial Co Ltd (in charge of operations such as SF Best and Heike) in 2015. Wang said: "In the future, we will participate and be deeply involved in various industries instead of being limited to 'last mile logistics,' for the latter will never make us deep-rooted in any industry." Wang, then CEO of SF Express, emphasized at various meetings on sales performance that SF Express should not only be an express delivery company but should also get involved in gaining new profits and extending into new business on the basis of the express delivery business.

Based on this, SF Express not only set forth to establish e-commerce platforms and offline retail stores but also set foot in cross-border e-commerce platform construction. In 2015, SF Haitao (now renamed as Fengqu) came into being. As a cross-border e-commerce supply chain platform, it tried to adopt a customized direct mail mode for non-standard products.

Giving full play to SF Express's advantages in logistics and supply chains, this new business mode aimed to compete for cross-border e-commerce market share. In spite of its ambitions, it encountered problems similar to those of other cross-border e-commerce enterprises. In the process of continuous development, problems such as fake goods, false advertisement, unauthorized cancellation of orders and inconvenience of returning goods were repeatedly exposed by the media.

In the fierce competition with its rivals, Fengqu has been blocked and almost strangled by Tmall Global, JD Worldwide, NetEase Kaola and other giants. Compared with Tmall Global, which boasts a market share of 27.8%, Fengqu's achievements were almost negligible.

According to a quarterly monitoring report on China's cross-border import retail in the e-commerce market published by Analysys International, in the first quarter of 2018, the market share of Fengqu accounted for only 1.1% of the whole, ranking ninth among its competitors.

TAKING ADVANTAGE OF THE FRANCHISE MODE AGAIN

In order to make SF Best more competitive, SF Express gave up its own regular chains mode and adopted the franchising mode for SF Best. With the expansion of stores, franchisees needed to pay the rent and bear related labour costs, while SF Express provided the costs of decoration and supplies of goods.

Under the franchise mode, it is noteworthy that the franchisee must deposit ¥300,000 as a performance bond, which serves as a means of obligation to the franchiser.

However, when there is no breach of contract, the full amount of ¥300,000 should be refunded at the expiration date.

According to SF Express's plan, SF Best intended to set up 4,500 offline stores in 2019 and 10,000 offline stores within 2020–2021. In this regard, readers may wonder whether the franchise mode can meet SF Express's ambitious retailing strategy. Luo Dan, a logistics analyst at Northeast Securities, said in an interview: "Although this practice of attracting investment greatly reduces a company's business risks, it will be a real test of SF's ability to enact quality control." SF Best sells more than 200 categories of products, including snacks, imported liquors and wines, mineral water, seafood, quick-frozen staple food, rice, flour, grain and cooking oil.[38]

Cao Lei, director of the China E-Business Research Center, has said:

> *Targeted at high-end customers, SF can only locate its shops in upscale residential areas, where the rents are not cheap. Moreover, upscale communities are defined by people's limited ability to buy the residences, which means there is not a large number of potential consumers. This is a huge test for SF.*

According to Cao, 80% of the products that SF Best provides are foreign brands aimed at high-end customers. However, due to the insufficiency of online transactions at present, the sales cost of SF Best is still relatively high. So far, SF Express has made a lot of bold attempts in the field of retailing but without any outstanding performance, whether through its offline stores, fresh goods e-commerce or cross-border e-commerce.[39]

Luo Dan pointed out in an interview:

> *Although SF Express can connect many large and small firms along the business chain through its own advantages, what it can boast of mainly lies in its long-distance distribution mode, while its daily distribution capacity in retailing is not so prominent.*

In Luo's view, although SF Express has a strong distribution capacity, it lacks advantages when it comes to warehousing. The reason is that a company's competitiveness in e-commerce and retail is specifically reflected in its warehousing and distribution, which is exactly SF Express's weak point.

In an interview with the media, Li Chengdong, an e-commerce analyst, explained:

> *Logistics means service capability, not retailing capability. Retailing requires a capability in building supply chains, an insight into consumers' needs and other capabilities. SF retail does not have such core capabilities in retailing, which is the main reason why it has always failed in this sector of business.*

Nevertheless, Wang Wei, when he was CEO of SF Express, continued to endeavour to reinvigorate the potential of the company's logistics and commercial dynamics. He said: "That's why SF Express has been so occupied with e-commerce retailing … that is, branding of channels comes first, then branding of products with the support of branded channels." However, such expectations are still to be realized.

"WE NEED TO EXPLORE NEW PROFIT SOURCES AND EXTEND NEW BUSINESSES"

Undeniably, the repeated setbacks in the retail industry affected SF Express's overall strategy. Having already spun off the commercial sector just before SF Express went public, Wang had to start his company's commercial exploration. "We need to explore new profit sources and extend new business branches on the basis of the express business," Wang said at SF Holding's annual performance meeting in 2016.

INITIATING NEW BUSINESSES

In 2017, in recent years, more and more competitors had been vying for SF Express's market share, so Wang had to initiate new lines of business. According to its published financial statements, SF Holding's major sector (express business) was under fierce attack from competitors. In the early days after the company went public, the enthusiasm of its investors caused its stock price to soar and made it the most valuable express delivery company in China.

Unfortunately, soon afterwards, the share price underwent a rollercoaster-like sharp decline. In the first quarter of 2017, the shareprice reached a peak of ¥73.34. After a period of turbulence, it significantly declined. By 14 June 2018, it had fallen to ¥46.32, dropping by 36.8% when compared with its peak price, and more than ¥90 billion was wiped off SF Holding's market value.[40]

The decline of SF Holding in the capital market was related to its rivals' rapid growth. According to the statistical bulletin on the development of the postal industry published by the State Post Bureau in 2017, the volume of goods transported in the express delivery business in

China reached 40.6 billion pieces, with a year-on-year increase of 28%.

There is a big gap between the growth of SF Express and the average growth of the whole express industry. According to statistics provided by All-Weather Science and Technology, SF Holding's market share of the express industry in 2017 was only about 7.62% (a decrease of 0.63% from 8.25% in 2016). It was left far behind by ZTO Express, STO Express, YTO Express, Yunda Express and Best Express, whose market shares were 15.5%, 12.6%, 11.8%, 9.73% and 9.4%, respectively. SF Express, the former hegemon of the express business, had now retreated to number six among China's express enterprises, although SF Holding had achieved just over 3 billion express deliveries in 2017, with a year-on-year increase of 18.29% according to its 2017 financial report.

The direct cause of SF Holding's decline was that Best Express, STO Express, YTO Express, Yunda Express and ZTO Express had been listed one after another, and had been expanding smoothly after their successful financing. For example, on 6 June 2018, STO Express announced that it had invested about ¥240 million to merge Shenzhen's transit assets, about ¥350 million to acquire transit assets in Guangzhou and about ¥60 million to acquire transit assets in Changsha. The large-scale expansion of STO Express suggested that it was intending to gradually transform to use the mode of regular chains in these key urban transit centres.

Additionally, China Post (another of SF Express's many rivals) was planning to integrate the resources of the company EMS into its main business. And an old opponent of SF Express, YTO Express, had launched its own brand of regular chains – OTP Express – which aimed at the medium and high-end express markets and had the advantage of an aviation licence. This meant that YTO Express was directly competing with SF Express for the high-end business market.

Previously, in contrast to SF Express, the other major Chinese express companies (such as STO Express, YTO Express, Yunda Express and ZTO Express) had chosen the mode of franchising, which meant that they would only focus on the procedure of collecting deliveries, whereas their franchisees would focus on transferring, dispatching and delivering procedures. Over years of operation, express companies had seen the drawbacks of this mode and finally ended up increasing the proportion of their regular chain stores.

The second direct cause of SF Holding's decline was that new players, such as Cainiao and JD Logistics, had joined the express industry, making it more competitive. JD Logistics is considered to be a strong competitor of SF because of the strategy promoted by Liu Qiangdong, the founder of JD.com. In 2017, Liu said in an interview with China Central Television: "In the future, only JD and SF will be able to gain a foothold in domestic logistics." Although this was a bold prediction, it showed Liu's determination to divide the market with an equal rival.

In August 2018, JD announced that it had built a logistics and warehousing base totalling 2.5 million square metres, enlarging its total storage area in mainland China to 12 million square metres, with logistics assets worth billions of yuan. In comparison, up to 30 June 2018, SF Holding possessed a total land area of about 4,603 *mu* (approximately 3,068,667 square metres), a total planned construction area of 3,006,100 square metres, and a total construction area of 848,800 square metres. Its net book value of logistics resources was about ¥9.1 billion.[41]

More than that, as a new rival, JD Logistics had not only been involved in the personal express business of three metropolises (Beijing, Guangzhou and Shanghai) but had also competed on price. According to data from the JD Business Deliveries Project, the previous pricing strategy applied by JD for this project was "to make a discount according to the volume of commercial deliveries on the basis of SF's prices." Whether SF or JD, both were defending their territories.

As of 2019, SF continued to maintain its advantages in air transport, and the number of its full cargo fleet had exceeded 50, reaching the standard of medium-sized airlines. The new rival, JD, announced that its first full cargo plane successfully made its maiden flight on 6 November 2018.

While the growth rate gradually slowed, SF's rivals, including old ones such as STO Express, YTO Express, Yunda Express and ZTO Express, plus some stronger companies, were also joining the competition. In September 2017, Alibaba announced that it had invested ¥5.3 billion to increase its shares in Cainiao. This increased Alibaba's equity share from 47% to 51%. According to the valuation at that time, Cainiao's value reached ¥132.5 billion, which was close to SF's ¥144.5 billion in December 2018.

In May 2018, Jack Ma, founder of Alibaba, expressed that Cainiao would invest ¥100 million as a strategic move in the future to build a "National Intelligent Logistics Backbone Network." Later, he showed his determination: "If ¥100 billion is not enough, we shall invest more hundreds of billions, and most of it will be invested in logistics as much as we can."

MORE INVESTMENT IN THE HEAVY FREIGHT EXPRESS MARKET

The third reason for the decline of SF Holding was that its own mode of regular chains had led to a continuous rise of operating costs. Data shows that in 2017, the operating cost of SF Holding's express logistics sector had reached ¥56.6 billion, a year-on-year increase of 22.93% compared with 2016.

Among all the costs, the biggest is labour costs, which in SF can be sorted into outsourcing costs and wage costs. In 2017, the expenditure on these two items was ¥27.9 billion and ¥10.1 billion, respectively, accounting for more than 60% of the total.

The implementation of a new national social security policy in 2019 also cast a cloud over labour-intensive delivery companies. The listed express companies were sure to bear the brunt. Sinolink Securities predicted that the net profit decrease of express companies such as Best Express, STO Express, YTO Express, Yunda Express and ZTO Express, caused by the impact of the new policy, would range between 5% and 10% on average. The 2017 annual SF Holding report showed that the total amount spent on employee wages was ¥136,000, and salaries of high-ranking executives accounted for a large proportion of the whole system. The market was quite concerned that the new social security regulations would have a very unfavourable impact.[42]

Yang Daqing, a contract researcher at the China Logistics Association, stated:

> *Nowadays, the express industry is shaped by advanced technologies. With unmanned technologies underway, the express industry as a labour-intensive industry will be transformed into a capital-intensive and technologically-intensive one. If SF fails to make a timely adjustment in the advancement of AI technologies,*

its 400,000-plus employees (according to SF's financial report, the number includes regular, dispatched and outsourcing employees) will become a huge burden.

Faced with these challenges, Wang Wei accelerated his pace of business development in such sectors as heavy freight express, intra-city distribution and other businesses, while expanding into new retail business.

On 12 May 2018, SF launched a strategic cooperation project with Xinbang Logistics and jointly held the Brand Launch and Partner Recruitment Conference in Guangzhou, making inroads into the LTL express market through the franchising model.

Sun Yan, a logistics analyst at Northeast Securities, told the media that the then current market scale of heavy freight express in China had reached ¥1.1 trillion, more than twice the size of the express business, which was ¥500 billion. He stated: "Although Deppon Express has been a leader in the express sector, this industry features a low concentration of market shares (Deppon Express has less than 2% of the market), which is an opportunity for SF."

In Sun's view, more investment in the heavy freight express market was a chance for SF to improve its competitiveness. Yang Daqing also mentioned in an interview: "The express market is sure to encounter more formidable challenges in the future. SF needs to keep on upgrading itself and trying to break through the barrier." He emphasized that more effort should be placed on constructing an AI network for warehousing and distribution, and that it was necessary to seek new space for survival of the express industry in the logistics market through investing in the new retailing and manufacturing industries. In addition, the acquisition of high-quality service providers was an important option to help SF make breakthroughs in its growth.

VENTURING INTO THE RETAIL SECTOR, DETERMINED TO WIN

Wang Wei's retail business, especially his e-commerce business, can be dated back as early as 2011. In that year, he set up SF Best online, expecting to realize the dream offered by the retail business. Unfortunately, SF Best's mediocre performance failed to meet the company's strategic targets. Yet, Wang did not give up his plan. In 2014, Wang began to set up Heike convenience stores all over mainland China, except Qinghai Province and Tibet. There were 518 stores in the first batch of openings, and by the end of 2014 SF had established nearly 3,000 Heike stores. This definitely proved Wang's determination to expand into the retail business.

However, real products were not initially presented in Heike stores. Customers only saw QR codes on the walls. When they needed to buy something, they could only place an order by scanning the QR code and then getting the product afterwards. As a result, the Heike stores didn't become popular despite huge investment.

Later, as previously outlined, the Heike stores were renamed SF Home and were integrated with SF Best. On 30 September 2015, SF Holding transferred 100% of the equity of SF E-commerce and SF Commerce to SF Holding Group Trading Co Ltd. The transfer price was ¥1.

On 30 May 2016, Dingtai New Material Co Ltd announced that the net profits of SF Holding's offload businesses were -¥126 million, -¥614 million and -¥866 million in 2013, 2014 and 2015, respectively, mainly because of their relatively large investments in the early stages. Also, there was a big change between 2013 and 2014, which was due to the fact that

SF Commerce began to set up offline stores at a quick pace in 2014, leading to a sharp increase in related costs.[43]

By the end of 2017, Wang was still continuing his exploration of the retail business and launched a project to offer self-service vending of snacks (E-nough Foods). At the 2017 SF annual meeting, Wang reflected on the previous failures:

> *SF has made abundant innovations and changes in the past two or three years, giving many of our employees in strategic departments a hard time. Our colleagues from different business groups had to deal with various difficulties, due to the constant change to our organizational structures. I am really sorry for that. Many people have left SF because of this. Everything seems to be normal from an outsider's perspective, but great changes have taken place inside our company.*

In 2017, the revenue of SF Commerce was only ¥79 million, with a year-on-year increase of 287.1%, but its costs grew as high as 302.9%.

Wang did not give up his experiments after this series of failures. This is exemplified by the frequent personnel changes in the CEO post of SF Best.

On 26 September 2018, Quan Guoshan became the CEO of SF Commerce. He was to be fully responsible for the daily management, strategic planning, business operation and other matters of SF Best, among other business groups. As a senior manager with more than 30 years' experience of cross-industry business operation, Quan was previously a senior manager in retail business (including supermarkets, superstores, department stores, home decor and e-commerce) as well as in the marketing and service industries, and had served several of the world's top 500 enterprises, including A.S. Watson (part of Hutchison Whampoa), Walmart, Home Depot, B&Q and Dairy Farm International Holdings (part of Jardine Matheson). He had also worked as a professional mentor in the Hong Kong Retail Management Association and as co-chair of the European Chamber of Commerce in Taiwan.[44]

Facing the aforementioned difficulties in the retail business, Wang decisively invited Quan to be his business partner, which obviously reflected his expectations. It was still SF's strategy to continue its expansion into new businesses. In April 2017, Wang said at a roadshow about the company's performance: "SF's future will lie in its involvement in many industries, and it will become specialized in many industries. We will not be limited to 'last mile' distribution, which will not make any further progress, but will use technologies to improve the whole industry. This is SF's future direction."

BUILDING A FULL-CHANNEL ECOLOGY OF BUSINESS

In March 2018, a commercial rivalry was launched between Meituan and DiDi. Meituan was a specialized fast-food delivery company and had more than 600 million users, while the specialized taxi service provider DiDi had 450 million users. The reason was that on 21 March 2018, the taxi service project Meituan Dache was officially launched in Shanghai after obtaining a licence to operate in Hangzhou, the capital of Zhejiang Province. Not to be outdone by Meituan, DiDi quickly launched the DiDi Delivery app to march into the delivery business.

At the time of writing, neither Meituan Dache nor DiDi Delivery had lived up to their expectations, but they do provide a case for further study. In the era of Internet+, the all-channel business mode remains popular among Chinese enterprises, including DiDi, Meituan and SF, because only those that dominate the all-channel market will have a say in China.

Taking another look at the above-mentioned competition, the overlap ratio between Meituan and DiDi app users reached an astonishing 19.46%. Such a high overlap ratio means a high conversion rate between the two apps. This was why Wang Wei was so eager to enter the retail market and tried to build an all-channel business ecosystem despite repeated setbacks.

According to Wang's strategic vision, SF was increasingly trying to activate all types of resources, including commerce, logistics, channels and finance. The destination was to realize the company's business blueprint by providing customers with customized business solutions.

A FULL-CHANNEL ECOLOGICAL ENVIRONMENT

Currently, there are two enterprises that have triumphed in the ecosystem-based construction of business: one is Apple Inc and the other is Xiaomi Corporation in China. Jia Yueting, the founder of LeEco, is a follower of Steve Jobs and has been striving to explore the idea of the business ecosystem in his own mind despite its many difficulties, putting forward a so-called "chemical reaction of ecological businesses" strategy. He made the following speech while attending the LETV annual meeting at LETV Ecological Sports Center in Beijing:

> *On their journey to the ecological world of business, I hope every LETVer is determined to forge ahead, since only the brave can truly appreciate the magnificence of this new world.*

It is no exaggeration to say that 2015 has witnessed a milestone for LETV. In the past year, we defined the future with the future per se, and then the present with the newly defined future. Relying on the new ecological model of the internet, we have kept on breaking through boundaries and witnessing the chemical reactions of ecological business. We have forged ahead bravely, fulfilling one promise after another to create a new economic form – the internet ecological economy. There are three major characteristics of this ecological economy, namely, value reconstruction, sharing and globalization. The destination is to form a complete ecosystem composed of closed vertical ecological chains and opened-up horizontal ecological circles.

In 2015, LETV has witnessed its initial success in the ecological economy. With more than 20 million paying members, LETV has become an internet enterprise with the highest individual value for its membership. The total revenue of the company has exceeded ¥20 billion, and the total ecological valuation has exceeded ¥300 billion. Among these achievements, the internet and cloud ecosystem businesses have become a surprise hit, making LETV Cloud the best brand of global video cloud and ecological cloud. LETV Mall has made its way into the first tier of the industry.

As for the service content, self-made products have become a dominating power. In competition with TCL, more than 3 million Super TV sets have been sold, beating all foreign TV brands and making this the number one brand in the market. LETV's Super Mobile Phones were the biggest dark horse of 2015, with over 5 million units shipped in 245 days. Consequently,

> *LETV has taken a stake in Coolpad Group and implemented an opened-up ecological strategy.*
>
> *We have completed the strategic layout of internet financing and have built our team for it; LETV Sports now ranks first in the industry, and our Series B financing is nearly complete. The Super car has completed its strategic layout, with top talents joining our forces. Product definition, as well as the basic research and development of the first generation of Super car, have been completed. So we have arrived at the painstaking stage of production preparation …*
>
> *With the joint efforts of all LETVers, a solid foundation has been laid for the globalization of LETV. A shared ownership for all employees and the implementation of a global partnership plan are attracting more and more global leaders in various industries to join the LETV ecosystem.*

Jia knew too well the difficulty of building a business ecosystem. In this speech, he admitted that there was no such thing as 'easy' in the ecological world of business. He reviewed his own path of development:

> *Over the past year, we have achieved unprecedented success. However, the road of reform and innovation in the ecological economy is bound to be painstaking and will inevitably be resisted or pressured by vested interests. Therefore, there is no such thing as 'easy' in the ecological world.*
>
> *To conquer the world, we must never cease to create brand new values! It is necessary to break free from common sense, conventions and traditions. It is also*

necessary to innovate in all aspects and throughout the whole process, and create brand new values in every dimension. So, the difficulties and resistance we are facing are tremendous, but I believe no one can beat us except ourselves.

We are facing insufficient supplies of capital. The internal reason for this problem is that we hope to leave the equity to the employees who are growing together with LETV's ecosystem, so that they can share the ecological values. The external reason is that only a few people can understand the complexity and advancement of LETV's ecosystem.

The development of the internet in China during the past 20 years is but a history of replication! It has just copied the successful model of the US, without any idea of innovation. Therefore, LETV's ecological model, which is original in a global sense, is not understood by others, but we will justify its cause with our efforts and results.

Strategy determines the method of organization, and organization leads to success. This is the second difficulty we are facing on our road to the ecological world. If the organization cannot innovate continuously, and the organization cannot be truly ecological, our ecological integration will face great challenges. In addition, we also need to strengthen the chemical reactions between organizations and coordinate closely with other ecosystems around the world.

Despite many obstacles on the way to the ecological world, no one can stop us from forging ahead. As long as all LETVers keep this solidarity and prioritize the interests of users all the time, we are sure to overcome all difficulties, to provide excellent ecological services for global users and to enjoy their applause.

Several other Chinese entrepreneurs – such as Lei Jun, founder of the Xiaomi Corporation, and Wang Wei – are also exploring paradigms of ecological construction in their respective business worlds.

National Business Daily reported on Wang's notion of ecological building:

Together with SF Buy (a platform of SF for cross-border shipment), SF Pay, a third-party payment platform through which consumers can pay for shipments, made a low-profile appearance in May 2014. In the same year, Shunyin Finance (part of SF) was developing into an infrastructural division, providing value-added services for the whole life cycle of express delivery. Thus, a cross-border ecosystem of SF, which integrated logistics, information flow and cash flow, was taking shape.

Some insiders commented that the integration of cash flow, information flow and logistics was the ultimate goal that Wang Wei pursued. In the blue oceans of cross-border business, SF intends to provide its international business partners with solutions featuring a global supply chain that includes cross-border logistics, full-channel sales, operational promotion and local customer services.[45]

As for SF Commerce, its structure has been streamlined into two parts. The first is an online e-commerce platform – SF Best. In order to better perform its role as an online e-commerce platform, SF Best has worked together with the company's offline community stores, aiming to build an efficient business system to provide all-channel services.

The second is offline community stores – SF Home and Heike. SF Home and Heike are intended to not only improve the customer experience but also solve the 'last mile' problem. At the same time, they provide customers with selected foods in season, global commodities, overseas online shopping services for maternal and infant supplies, quality day-to-day goods, express logistics and all kinds of convenience services. In this way, these offline stores can provide quality products and services for community customers and effectively meet their needs.

Li Dongqi, the vice president of SF Group and the president of SF Commerce, explained in an interview: "SF Commerce should be regarded as a whole, and in that way SF Group is able to integrate its online and offline resources. We want to be a full-channel operator that includes commodity sales, transportation and services to promote residential community consumption."

In Li's view, the commercial ambitions of SF and its strategic layout can be realized by the company's commerce business group through its cultivation of a full-channel ecological environment: "The integration of online and offline resources, combined with services such as delivery, cold chain transport and financing, can help various firms to fully connect with their end customers."

By integrating relevant channels, SF can even provide different firms with couriers for direct sales in the future. Li told the media: "There are 210,000 couriers in SF, who in total can reach 10 million customers within a day. This is a very important channel. Frankly speaking, SF Business plays a leading role at every link in the circulation within Internet+."

COMMUNITY DISTRIBUTION AS A SOLUTION TO THE 'LAST MILE' PROBLEM

Incurring costs is almost unavoidable in exploring a new business form, and this is especially true in offline business. Heike has been criticized harshly by researchers, media and commentators since its initiation because of its sparse customer flow, problematic business model and many other problems.

In response to this situation, Li Dongqi said:

> *Although Heike is not perfect, it is a necessary stage in the development of SF Commerce. The success of Heike lies in the fact that it has installed collection and delivery services within residential communities, thus extending logistics into these communities. Only on this basis are we able to enhance our commercial and service functions. One of the problems in e-commerce, which has been solved by Heike, is how to cope with delivery by appointment. The strategic significance of Heike, which is often neglected by outsiders, is much more important to us than the current gains and losses. The industry is well aware of the costs of end-to-end distribution. Without these stores, it would be empty talk to claim that we had solved the 'last mile' problem in delivery. What would be the use of that?*

In Li's opinion, the ongoing competition in the express industry cannot be compared with those in the past. Therefore, a tougher competitive stance will be needed to win in the future. He said:

> *We could not make it in the absence of offline stores. If SF Commerce is endowed with more commercial*

functions, customers' experience is sure to be improved, so we really need physical stores to achieve this. With these stores, we will see infinite possibilities under the derivative functions of commerce. For example, some customers will ask whether SF Commerce can provide feedback within one week after a transaction. This will only be possible when we have optimized our offline stores to increase consumers' trust and fulfil these demands.

Therefore, as previously mentioned, SF Express launched SF Home, which is actually a second iteration of Heike. According to Li, its purpose is to "transform to a more commercial and service-oriented model with enhanced functions based on the needs of the community." It is undeniable that rather than waiting passively for a better chance to march into the offline business, SF Express has actively carried out a transformation by itself. In an article titled "Innovation and Change: From 'SF Express' to 'SF Service,'" Wang Wei wrote:

In the past two years, I have been talking about 'transformation' very frequently. Compared with the past years, when we mainly focused on the express business, there are indeed many new businesses in the landscape of SF Express.

In June 2012, SF Best, which mainly focuses on medium and high-end foods, was launched, marking SF's big move into the e-commerce field. In 2013, SF initiated Heike, a brand of residential community stores that soon covered most regions of the country. At the same time, SF added several business groups such as e-commerce and supply chains. In addition, it has provided more integrated services, including express logistics, e-commerce logistics, auto-mobility logistics, food and medical transport services, financial and insurance services, and international e-commerce services, hoping to provide one-stop integrated logistics solutions for customers.

As a matter of fact, SF has no previous experience in the business of contract logistics, which in my view is a must now, because the needs of some large group customers have changed. They want to straighten out the entire supply chain by outsourcing all their logistics services from one reliable logistics company. We should refer to the organizational structures and business models of today's four international express giants for our medium and long-term development. Now in China, the logistics industry has been accustomed to a decentralized business model – one supplier for domestic commodities, another supplier for express, and still another for warehousing and e-commerce distribution. But this will change in the near future. Therefore, we must now invest resources to prepare as well as we can for the change.

Our goal is that, in five years, we will make our customers understand our new service concept and acknowledge that SF is not just an express company. When they think of SF, they will call it SF Service instead of SF Express.

Next, SF will create a 'logistics department store' concept. 'Customers come with needs, and SF provides solutions.' This is the goal we must achieve in the future.[46]

To Wang, the core value of SF Express is 'service' rather than 'express.' This is a voluntary choice rather than passive acceptance of the company's fate.

CHAPTER 7

A TRANSFORMATION INTO THE REALM OF LOGISTICS REAL ESTATE

In the past two years, I have been talking about 'transformation' very frequently. Compared with the past years, when we mainly focused on express operations, there are indeed many new businesses in the landscape of SF Express.

– Wang Wei

SUPPLY CHAIN FINANCE

Alongside its large-scale development, SF Express, as if suffering from a midlife crisis, has begun to experience a painful process of growth. Describing the process of its transformation, media reports have straightforwardly described its situation as "SF's Midlife Crisis" and "SF's Transitional Pain," also referring to "Unblessed SF."

Such media comments were based on SF Express's unsatisfactory half-year earnings and its stock price. Some experts even wrote: "Its income growth cannot keep up with its cost growth." Faced with such a situation, Wang Wei, while reducing various company costs, was actively looking for new areas of profit growth. Supply chain finance began to attract his attention.

In 2015, Wang began to set foot in supply chain finance, one of the new businesses that he betted on. Certainly, his involvement in supply chain finance was based on SF Express's core features.

As mentioned earlier, Wang founded SF Holding in Guangdong in 1993. As of 2019, its scale had grown a great deal, and it had established regional distribution centres in Beijing, Shanghai, Guangzhou, Chengdu, Wuhan, Shenyang and Xi'an, with hundreds of warehouses in

50 key cities, tens of thousands of distribution outlets, nearly 2 million square metres of storage area, and a coverage of 2,500 districts and counties in China.

This set of data suffices to show that the warehousing system built by Wang had an incomparable advantage over the company's competitors. Additionally, SF has improved its efficiency through accruing information and introducing high-tech and advanced equipment, which has effectively decreased the number of errors caused by manual operation. By applying an automatic sorting system, it has reduced its dependence on manual work. By tracing the transportation process through the Global Positioning System (GPS), SF is able to configure and adjust cargo transportation, thus optimizing the use of vehicles and reducing excessive vehicle purchase costs.

In Wang's view, it is crucial to constantly improve the company's infrastructure, systematically optimize its network construction, develop and apply new technologies and equipment, and effectively apply these technologies and equipment to process management. This process includes, for example, sections of customer services, collecting and dispatching, warehousing, transportation and customs declaration – in other words, the whole life cycle of delivered goods.

With its warehousing and distribution network, which covers the whole country, and its high degree of information management, SF possesses a large quantity of B-terminal and C-terminal customer data and relatively complete logistics, capital and information flow.[47] This provides strategic support for Wang's involvement in supply chain finance.

THE BUSINESS MODE OF SUPPLY CHAIN FINANCE

In 2015, under Wang Wei's guidance, SF Group set up a business group for financial services and formally established a department of supply chain finance. This was not the first time that SF had been involved in supply chain finance. Zhang Hui, director of SF's supply chain finance department, said in an interview: "SF actually participated in logistics finance as early as around 2013 in the form of collection on delivery, which is the starting point for most logistics companies aiming to carry out supply chain finance."

Since then, the company has launched four modes of supply chain financing products: purchase order financing, accounts receivable factoring financing, warehousing pledges and credit loans.

First, purchase order financing. It is understood that SF Express may provide its purchase order financing business to customers with whom the company has had a long-term cooperation. When such customers have signed sales contracts with their downstream customers, they may apply for order financing because they do not have enough funds to purchase raw materials for production. Subsequently, SF Express will pay the funds needed by its own customers. In addition, it can also provide warehousing, transportation and distribution of goods for its customers in the whole process.

Second, accounts receivable factoring. It is understood that SF Express mainly provides this service to partners that have receivables and payables within their supply chains. Certainly, SF Express has its own advantages in terms of the long duration, low threshold and low costs of this service. The specific process of operation is that, after SF Express buys out the customers' accounts receivable, the purchasing partner pays the money directly to the factoring company's account.

Third, warehousing pledges. It is said that the warehousing pledge business provided by SF Express was the earliest supply chain financial product that the company launched. It is mainly aimed at customers who stock up in SF warehouses in advance, and usually provides credit lines ranging from ¥1 million to ¥30 million to customers.

Zhang Chunhong, product manager of the supply chain finance department of SF Financial Services Group, once commented on this business mode: "This mode is related to the rapid development of e-commerce in recent years. Relying heavily on internet sales, e-commerce tends to choose a light asset mode, which makes it more difficult for them to obtain loans from banks, whereas SF warehousing financing can meet their needs."

Of course, in this business mode, customers can choose to make payments either before or after receiving goods. That is, they could apply for a loan first, pledge the goods purchased with the loan to SF Express's warehouse service, and then use the sales proceeds to repay the loan. Alternatively, they could pledge the goods to SF's warehouse service for a further loan and use the sales proceeds to repay the initial loan. SF Express warehouse financing also includes dynamic pledges. When the company began to provide financing loans to customers, the warehouse management system would monitor the daily inflow and outflow of customers' goods and the value of the remaining goods, and adjust the credit lines according to the dynamic records.[48]

Fourth, credit loans (or SF Small Loans). It is understood that the credit loans business provided by SF is mainly aimed at dealers of substantial economy or e-commerce corporate customers who have good cooperation with

SF and are engaged in commodity sales. In this business, SF usually provides these enterprises with credit loans ranging from ¥50,000 to ¥1 million.

RISK CONTROL

It is undeniable that any express delivery enterprise involved in supply chain finance must manage its risk well. Chu Xuejian, executive deputy director of the Modern Logistics Research Center at Shanghai University, stated: "It will be a trend for logistics enterprises to develop the business of supply chain finance, but they need to have a strong sense of risk control, such as the selection of collateral, value assessment, liquidation point selection, and control of the flow of goods."

In Chu's view, risk control would determine whether SF's supply chain finance would succeed or not. Such being the case, how has SF reduced the risks in its supply chain finance?

First, in order to better control risks, SF has completed the design of financial products encompassing the whole supply chain, by referring to transaction data, logistics data, system docking and the company's rating monitoring system.

Second, SF has referred to big data analyses and applications by some mainstream platforms, and has investigated how traditional banks have carried out their risk control and designed their scoring systems. In this way, SF has learned how to improve on these models and apply them to its own products.

Third, SF has applied its unique risk control strategy according to different financing modes. For example, in the warehousing pledge business, much attention is paid to the customer's purchase information and payment information, as well as to the evaluation and inspection of incoming merchandise. It is also necessary to manage and control the storage and transportation of these customers' goods. Another example can be found in the factoring financing business: SF needs to conduct a thorough study of the supply relationship and supply cycle between the two sides, and analyse and verify the multi-dimensional data.

Obviously, SF enjoys its own advantages in terms of risk control. The role it plays determines its degree of involvement in inventory management and mainline transportation at the front end, and terminal distribution as well. Thus, Song Hua, an expert at a Chinese logistics financial think tank, stated:

> *Logistics belongs to a passive third-party industry, the core of which is goods. Delivery companies can only realize the sustainable development of supply chain finance after they have in hand the data of cooperative customers, such as operating products, the popularity of products, market distribution and customer maintenance. Then they can provide customized warehousing and distribution services, and finally get linked with the industrial chain.*

In Song's view, customized warehousing, transportation and distribution services are key points to ensure the sustainable development of supply chain finance. These services are also SF's greatest advantage in this area.

In order to effectively control risk, SF tried to achieve its technological breakthrough by means of a strategic alliance. In April 2018, SF announced that SF Holding and Tongdun Technology would jointly establish Beijing Shunhetongxin Technology Co Ltd. Information about Tongdun can be found on the company's official website:

> *Tongdun Technology Co Ltd, founded in 2013 and headquartered in Hangzhou, Zhejiang Province, is a professional provider of intelligent risk control, analysis and decision-making services in China. Tongdun adheres to the concept of AaaS (intelligent analysis as a service) risk control. It combines AI with business scenarios, thus providing services for more than ten industries, such as banking, insurance, auto finance, non-bank credit, funds, tripartite payments, electricity, air travel, O2O [online to offline], games and social networking platforms. Its services include smart marketing, smart credit risk control, AI anti-fraud, AI operation, etc. So far, more than 10,000 enterprise customers have chosen Tongdun's products and services.*
>
> *While highly trusted by its clients, Tongdun Technology has also been praised by the media, investment communities and various industries both in China and abroad. The company has completed five rounds of fundraising and has accumulated hundreds of millions of dollars of investment.*
>
> *Tongdun has clinched numerous accolades, including Best Cloud-Based Application in 2017 (awarded by The Asian Banker), the 2015 Red Herring Global Top 100 in Technology Innovation, Forbes China's FinTech 50, 2017 KPMG China's FinTech 50, Asia Money China's Leaders in FinTech, China AI's Top 50 (unveiled at the World Economic Forum, commonly known as the Summer Davos Forum), the Ram*

Charan Management Practice Award, and CSR [Corporate Social Responsibility] Rising Star (unveiled at China's Corporate Social Responsibility 100 Forum). Last but not least, it has marched into some prestigious lists, such as the 2018 World AI Industry Development Blueprint (published by Gartner) and the 2018 CB Insights Global FinTech Unicorns list.

Tongdun Technology has offices in Hangzhou, Beijing, Shanghai, Shenzhen, Guangzhou, Chengdu, Xi'an, Chongqing, Singapore and Jakarta. Over 80% of the members of Tongdun's team are veterans in AI, cloud computing, risk management, anti-fraud, business decision-making and other professional fields. Tongdun Technology hopes to leverage the three core technology systems of AI, big data analytics and cloud computing to empower the financial, internet, logistics, medical, retail and other industries to establish an intelligent business decision-making platform, and finally realize the vision of "Intelligent Decision-Making Life Better."[49]

From this introduction, we can see that Tongdun Technology has a good reputation in anti-fraud and intelligent risk control. That is why SF chose Tongdun to jointly establish Shunhetongxin Technology Co Ltd and to explore in depth the data value of logistics, information flow and capital flow. The purpose was to provide risk control and data analysis products and services for the logistics industry, the retail industry and the supply chain finance industry. Moreover, together with another eight supply chain enterprises (such as Eternal Asia), SF has jointly established a large supply chain data platform to build an efficient and collaborative intelligent supply chain system. It was suggested in 2018 that this would definitely improve the company's competitiveness.[50]

TRANSFORMATION AND OPTIMIZATION

One reason that many companies are reluctant to transform is that they are obsessed with their previous successes. Kodak, for example, was the first company in the world to develop digital photography technology, yet it was eventually beaten by Japanese digital companies because of its unwise adherence to the film production business. Zhang Jindong, founder of the Chinese electronics giant Suning Appliance Group, commented: "The biggest obstacle to business transformation is that many people are obsessed with their past success."

Zhang's caution was derived from his own management practices. One scholar spoke highly of Suning (among other companies):

> *Suning once ranked first among private enterprises, Haier is a leader of household appliances in China, while Wanda is the benchmark of commercial real estate. These enterprises were formed in the 1980s after China's reform and opening-up, and they were the earliest beneficiaries of the dividends of reform. Studies have found that as long as enterprises do not experience transitional crises, they are unaware that they are just at the top of a parabolic curve. This could have been the case for all three. Success can be exciting, but it can also be a burden of transformation – this is a truth for almost everyone. However, there exists a phenomenon of 'self-anaesthesia,' also known*

as 'pretended sleeping,' which is common among disparate groups of people and institutions.

Indeed, every time such a giant company undergoes a transition, it is undoubtedly very difficult, especially when it has already climbed to the top of the curve. The three companies mentioned above faced the same problem in their transformation. Restrained by their own success, while taking into consideration their industrial advantages, they needed to learn how to get rid of these heavy burdens. In that sense, the biggest obstacle is not uncertainty about the unknown but the success of the past. It was exactly under such circumstances that Wang Wei initiated SF's reform attempt and thus kicked off its initiative of transformation and optimization.

INTERNAL AND EXTERNAL FACTORS OF CHANGE

In the express industry, discussions are always focused on the merits and disadvantages of the regular chains mode and the franchising mode. Of course, this debate affected the reform and transformation of SF Express.

Considering the drastic changes in the market environment, Wang Wei and his executives had to address such problems as how to adapt to the business mode of the Internet+ era and enable SF to maintain the same rate of development that it had seen in its first 20 years.

According to Xu Qian, vice president of SF Group and president of the East China region of SF Express, the company's future development was concerned with two aspects. First, some external factors needed to be addressed, such as the in-depth development of globalization, the new economic wave and the evolving state of the express industry itself.

Second, there were some significant internal factors. After more than 20 years of development, SF had acquired its own competitive advantages. In its reform, it needed to carefully weigh the pros and cons of each move, including such factors as circumstances, customers and self-development.

SF had formed a network management model based on the integration of different business sectors. Xu's judgement was based on his unique perspective from his experience before he joined SF in 2016. Prior to this, Xu had worked in the banking industry, serving Standard Chartered Bank (CB) from 2003 and Deutsche Bank from 2007. In July 2016, he joined SF as an assistant CEO.

Xu concluded that:

> *Over the past 25 years, along with the expansion of the market, the layout of depots, the demands of customers and SF's specific demands relating to distribution and bulk cargo management, the company has come all the way from southern China to the east, the north, the midwest and other regions as well. It has gradually formed a management model based on the disparity of each single region.*

The formation of SF's network management model originated within its process of development, which is quite clear when you look back at its history. SF started in southern China and now it has developed into a courier enterprise covering almost all cities above the county level in China.

This development also meant that, in the process of expansion, SF needed to become more and more specific about its target customers, because different services are required by different industries in different regions. Therefore, it needed varying regional management. Thus, over a period when other express delivery companies were building their own networks on a large scale, SF set up a framework of more than 60 business regions.

In order to match its competitors' development, SF began to improve itself by further dividing up its regions into units while reforming and optimizing its system for piecework commissions. In an interview with the media, Xu stated:

> *The advantages of the regional management model are obvious. To name just a few, it can help a company to understand the situation of specific regions, integrate the corporate policies with the local environment and manage the investment of various resources. But at the same time, some drawbacks have also been exposed – for example, there might be interest conflicts between different regions.*

Xu also stated:

> *At the same time, this mode has caused disconnections between regional operating frameworks, customer service systems, pricing systems and the actual needs of customers. Sometimes, we do not provide a delivery service to our customers in the best way. On other occasions, we fail to invest our resources where they should go. As a result, some regions will only look after their own local interests and forget the company's common interests. Some regions will be obsessed with developing their own customers, forgetting to share the resources with other regions, while other regions will just focus on SF Group's*

allocation of resources, forgetting the actual needs of customers. Not to mention the stagnation of talent flow and so on. Therefore, an experimental system of integrated operation has been adopted in Jiangsu, Zhejiang, Shanghai and Anhui provinces, to try to overcome these shortcomings and solve these problems. The customers do not see the business unit or regional divisions of SF. All they can see are SF and SF's services.

AN ATTEMPT AT A ZONING SYSTEM

At present, there exist many controversies around the regular chains mode and the franchising mode, both of which have commonly been applied in the express logistics industry. SF Express, which ultimately adopted the regular chains mode, has always relied on an asset-heavy strategy and has inevitably purchased a large number of movable and immovable assets, which has invited much criticism.

However, my opinion is opposite to that of many researchers. Personally, I believe that SF Express's asset-heavy mode will be the key to it winning against the competition in the future. Owing to this mode, SF Express can provide customers with the best services. Although the franchise system can reduce the costs of the whole process and maintain strong flexibility, it also has many drawbacks.

The regular chains mode actually dwarfs the franchise mode in such areas as the efficient execution of headquarters' decisions, unified services and competitive pricing. However, the disadvantages of regular chains are also obvious. For example, the whole system is much bigger, there are high costs from the movable and immovable assets and other aspects, and some barriers intentionally result from the design.

To overcome the disadvantages of the regular chains mode, Xu Qian's solution was to turn them into advantages. The newly adopted zoning system was an effective method the company adopted to solve the problems existing in SF's regional management mode. "This doesn't mean the abolition of regional divisions," Xu said. "For different regions, the new system is intended to achieve an effect of 1 + 1 > 2."

According to Xu, the 16 business regions of SF Express in East China were regrouped into five major zones: Shanghai, southern Jiangsu (including cities such as Suzhou, Wuxi, Changzhou and Nantong), the Jiangsu–Anhui zone (including Nanjing, northern Jiangsu, southern Anhui and northern Anhui), northern Zhejiang (including Jiaxing, Hangzhou, Shaoxing and Ningbo), and southern Zhejiang (including Wenzhou, Jinhua and Taizhou).

The original intention of implementing the zoning system was to realize medium- and long-term development in East China. The idea was that the interactions between these zones, their common policy, their resource sharing and their collaborative development could effectively optimize the allocation of resources.

Xu explained that the systemic reorganization through this Jiangsu–Zhejiang–Shanghai–Anhui integration was the first step of SF Express improving the overall competitiveness of these 16 regions in East China. To decide which areas should be grouped together, the company considered the ability of the regions to coordinate and synergize. He explained:

> *For example, Nanjing, northern Jiangsu, southern Anhui and northern Anhui are integrated into one single zone to optimize our operation. Prior to this regrouping, parcels from Anhui Province had to be first*

> *sent to its capital city, Hefei, and then to Xuzhou and other cities in Jiangsu Province. Now, with the new operation mode, the parcels from Anhui Province can be sent directly to Xuzhou, which has brought obvious effects in both cost reduction and efficiency improvement. Therefore, it was appropriate to regroup these four separate regions into one.*

Xu stated that the allocation of resources in different regions must be fully utilized. For example, if the resources in Suzhou, Wuxi, Changzhou and Nantong were fully utilized, southern Jiangsu (the region they represented) could benefit more from the operation model updates and its warehouse construction, and would better support Shanghai. Likewise, the newly established zone of northern Zhejiang (including Jiaxing, Ningbo, Shaoxing and Hangzhou) has a higher economic vitality as a result of the changes. Once the resources within the same zone are fully utilized, there are considerable benefits. Another example is the southern Zhejiang zone (including Jinhua, Taizhou and Wenzhou), which has a large output of fresh Chinese bayberry. If the regions within the zone were to set up common standards and prices for the fruit industry, they would undoubtedly be more competitive than before.

Of course, Shanghai plays a vital role in utilizing the resources of the northern Zhejiang and southern Zhejiang zones. Xu said: "Some of our customers locate their headquarters in Shanghai, while their production bases are in other regions. In such cases, Shanghai could help to be a driving force in improving their coordination."

Xu thinks that the zoning system is a bold attempt to solve the current problems of SF Express. Once the system is successfully implemented, the following three positive results can be expected.

First, there will be more efficient resource allocation. When the resources of all these regrouped regions are fully utilized, the company's investment will be mostly directed to meet the market and customers' demands, which will help to break through regional boundaries.

Second, SF's market competitiveness will be enhanced. In the past, each region had its own way of settling accounts. Consequently, parcels had to be transited several times to accommodate different operational rules. However, once the zoning system is activated, there will be fewer transits and higher loading rates, thus naturally increasing the efficiency.

Third, such arrangements will increase the flow and exchange of talents. In the past, the free exchange of talents could not be realized because of regional boundaries. After the adoption of the zoning structure, the personnel, financial and material resources will be fully utilized, which will readily promote talent exchange.

FURTHER EXPLORATION OF THE ZONING SYSTEM

The adoption of the zoning system has brought many new ideas to SF Express. The functioning of the East China zone has not only brought much collaborative thinking and many new initiatives into full play in the region but has also stirred up the enthusiasm of all regional directors, who commonly meet to brainstorm and elect the leader for each zone.

Xu Qian said: "In fact, East China has nurtured a good atmosphere of reform over the past year. The zoning system is not a whim, but has drawn on the wisdom of all 16 regions in East China. And its formation is based on a large amount of statistics, facts and research."

In Xu's opinion, the formation of the five major zones (containing the 16 regions) was based on the power of team spirit. Moreover, when this practice has solved the problem of business stratification, what will remain is the appointment of a new leader for all five zones. He said:

> *Whether Shanghai has the ability or any willingness to lead will be decided by further assessments. We should decide when and how to make use of existing performance mechanisms and talent pools, to help Shanghai to play the leading role. So, the empowerment of Shanghai is much more important than just making some requests.*

Xu holds that the zoning system is going to break the restraint of some existing frameworks and rules of SF Express in a bottom-up way. Throughout Chinese history, no matter when and how reforms happened, almost all were carried out in a top-down approach. This means they were dominated by the ruling class, such as Shang Yang's reforms in the State of Qin (in 356 BC and 350 BC), King Wuling's reforms in the State of Zhao (starting in 307 BC), Wang Mang's reform in the Xin dynasty (AD 9–23), Emperor Xiaowen's policy of Sinicization during the Northern Wei dynasty (472–499), the 'Two Wangs and Eight Supervisors of Military Affairs' reform (also referred to as the Yongzhen Reform) in the Tang dynasty (in 805), the New Policies in the Northern Song dynasty (1069–1085), Zhang Juzheng's reform in the Ming dynasty (1573–1582) and the Westernization movement in the Qing dynasty (1861–1895).

Here, we will review the background and achievements of Shang Yang's reforms. In the early Warring States period (475–221 BC), the economy and military power of Qin lagged behind the other six states, namely the states of Qi, Chu, Yan, Zhao, Wei and Han. Faced with the pressure of being defeated, Duke Xiao of Qin strove to elevate the status of Qin in the struggle for hegemony. Hence, he issued an announcement calling for men of talent to aid him in strengthening the state.

Subsequently, Shang Yang's reforms took place. These have influenced China for thousands of years. Fearing criticism by his subjects, the duke convened court meetings to discuss the matter. In the debate, Gan Long and Du Zhi, who represented the old nobles, denied the necessity of reform. They held that a reform should not be implemented if it would bring no more than 100 times the benefit of the current system. And a new utensil should not be used if its functions would be no more than ten times those of the old one. After all, "It would be no mistake to model oneself on the ancients [*fa gu*] and no harm would come from following the old rituals [*xun li*]."

Shang Yang responded defensively:

> *Which ancient laws should we abide by when each of the previous dynasties had their own institutions? Which kind of old rituals [*li*] should we follow when previous emperors and kings never repeated the way of their predecessors? We must not govern the state in one fixed way and copy the ancients. As long as the practice is beneficial to the state, we should complement it. Emperors Tang and Wu did not follow the ancient laws, yet they made their states prosperous. The old rituals were followed in the Shang and Xia dynasties, yet both ended in chaos. Therefore, those who oppose*

> *the ancient rituals are not necessarily wrong and those who follow are not necessarily right.*

In this way, Shang Yang advocated that "laws and decrees should be issued according to the times; rituals should be based on social reality." With this thinking about historical evolution, Shang Yang refuted the principles of *fa gu* (to model oneself on the ancients) and *xun li* (to follow the old rituals), which were advocated by the old aristocrats, and prepared well to publicize the reform.

After two phases of reform, the old system of Qin was completely abolished and the state witnessed an economic boom. After a period of development, it gradually became the most powerful state in the Warring States period, which laid a solid foundation for the later Qin Dynasty to unify all the other states in China.

There is no denying that reform is extremely important for both countries and enterprises. As Xu Qian said:

> *There is no experience from which we can learn about the zoning system. But as long as there are innovations and improvements in resource coordination, talent exchange and business cooperation, the benefits of the system should be recognized. At the same time, we need to ceaselessly explore and reflect, in order to finally set up a mature system.*

Xu had to admit that it would simply be impossible to rely on a single system, because each region has its own unique features. Nevertheless, SF Express has explored a new path in its development through technological innovation. Xu said:

When the zoning system is activated and supported by technology, whether it will be more effective to apply a broader mode of management will be left to SF Express itself to explore. Up to now, we haven't had any ready answer yet, since the overall technological capability of the company needs to be further tested. What about the future? The possibilities of the current times offer an irresistible pull!

BEING AN INTEGRATED LOGISTICS SERVICE PROVIDER

The nature of strategic transformations are often determined by an enterprise's own business features and scale, and SF Express is no exception.

SF Express, a company dedicated to building a comprehensive ecosystem, has not only actively diversified its business on the basis of express delivery but is also accelerating its pace of innovation, thus becoming a member of the industrial circle of new logistics. On the basis of this status, SF Express is intent on becoming an integrated logistics service provider under the principle of being "logistics based, financially integrated and interconnected in business."

Certainly, SF Express's involvement in logistics real estate is closely related to the acceleration of China's industrial upgrades and new urbanization. Logistics real estate served as a strategic breakthrough for SF Express, and this promoted the transformation and upgrading of regional industries by integrating natural, social and economic resources, thus effectively fuelling the economic growth of various regions.

INTO THE REALM OF LOGISTICS REAL ESTATE

As is commonly known, the rapid expansion of both e-commerce and the retail market may promote the construction of large manufacturing bases. This will undoubtedly serve as an engine for the rise of e-commerce and the improvement of logistics and storage facilities, playing a decisive role in the development of regional economies.

Faced with this situation, SF Express, as a leading enterprise in the express industry, has planted its feet in the realm of logistics real estate, in order to improve its capability to integrate its logistics service and explore a larger blue ocean market.

In 2013, SF Express established an operations centre for its industrial parks and expanded this mode nationwide through the strategy of 'self-construction + cooperation.' By 7 November 2018, SF Express had built 16 industrial parks in 34 cities. With these industrial parks, SF Express wished to activate and make good use of the company's internal and external resources, so as to effectively optimize their allocation.

On 6 September 2017, SF Express signed a strategic cooperation agreement with Vanke Logistics Real Estate at the Shenzhen Dameisha Vanke Group headquarters. According to their agreement, the two parties intended to strengthen their interaction and coordination, give full play to their complementary advantages, and seek strategic cooperation in logistics warehousing, cold chain exploration, smart parks and commercial facilities. At the same time, they would further explore some new models and opportunities for cooperation, so as to provide new ideas and solutions for the development and improvement of their urban facilities. They decided to cooperate in such areas as long-term lets, product innovation, central housekeeping, community entrances, smart parks and cold chain logistics.

On 11 September 2017, SF Express signed a "strategic partnership letter of intent" with Global Logistics Properties to deepen their collaboration in logistics transit, supply chain warehousing, cold chain development, logistics facilities and finance.

Then, on 14 November 2017, SF Express announced that it had signed a strategic cooperation agreement with Goodman to jointly develop and build warehouse facilities in the Hong Kong Special Administrative Region. By sharing knowledge and information, SF Express and Goodman would cooperate to ensure that SF Express had the best logistics and warehouse facilities.

In addition to the business giants mentioned above, SF Express has also agreed strategic cooperation with a number of well-known logistics real estate developers.

BUILDING LOGISTICS PARKS

One key reason for SF Express to strengthen the role of logistics real estate is to meet its own business needs. This is because the construction of logistics real estate is an imperative for improving efficiency and the links between each stage in logistics. This is also true for other express companies. Therefore, in order to gain more of a competitive advantage, in 2014 SF Express started to build logistics parks, expand its distribution centres and establish aviation logistics centres.

According to *China Post News*, other companies (including Ane Express, China Post, Deppon Logistics, JD Logistics, STO Express, YTO Express, Yunda Express and ZTO Express) have also been developing real estate, as shown in Table 7.1.

Company	Date	Location(s)	Project
SF Express	December 2014	Changzhou, Jiangsu	SF E-commerce Industrial Park
	January 2015	Taizhou, Jiangsu	SF E-commerce Industrial Park
	January 2016	Foshan, Guangdong	SF Integrated Industrial Park, including warehousing and refrigerated transportation
	April 2016	Ezhou, Hubei	SF Hubei International Logistics Hub
	December 2016	Weihai, Shandong	SF Weihai E-commerce Industrial Park
	December 2016	Wuhu, Anhui	SF Wuhu E-commerce Industrial Park
YTO Express	May 2015	Jining, Shandong	YTO modern distribution centre
	September 2016	Shanxi	Signed contracts to build a transit centre and airline base in northwest China
	2017	Jiaxing, Zhejiang	YTO Global Airline Logistics Hub and Airline Base
	Still in planning	Yiwu, Zhejiang	YTO Zhejiang headquarters, e-commerce industrial park, regional airline hub and logistics distribution centre
	Still in planning	Chengdu, Sichuan	YTO regional headquarters and international airline hub
STO Express	November 2014	Hangzhou, Zhejiang	Project to expand its distribution centre in East China
	March 2015	Quzhou, Zhejiang	Signed contract to build STO Longyou E-commerce Industrial Park
	May 2015	Xi'an, Shanxi	STO Northwest China Transit Center
	March 2016	Zhengzhou, Henan	Started to build its logistics distribution centre in Central China
	April 2016	Panshan, Liaoning	Transit centre, function management centre and automatic distribution centre in northeast China

Company	Date	Location(s)	Project
ZTO Express	July 2015	Ziyang, Sichuan	ZTO Ziyang E-commerce Industrial Park
	January 2016	Harbin, Heilongjiang	Signed contract to build ZTO Harbin Transit Center
	March 2016	Jinan, Shandong	Opened the Operation Center and Zhongtongji Logistics Project
	July 2016	Panjin, Liaoning	Built headquarters and achieved transit–distribution integration in northeast China
Yunda Express	May 2016	Ningbo, Zhejiang	Yunda Ningbo E-commerce Industrial Park
	December 2016	Taizhou, Jiangsu	Yunda Taizhou E-commerce Industrial Park
JD Logistics	December 2009	Shanghai	The Asia No. 1 Logistics Center
	December 2010	Wuhan, Hubei	JD Central China E-commerce District
	May 2013	Wuhan, Hubei	JD E-commerce Industrial Park
Deppon Logistics	May 2010	Foshan, Guangdong	Deppon Southwest Operation Center
	2010	Wuhan, Hubei	Deppon Central China Operation Center
	March 2016	Wuhan, Hubei	Deppon Logistics Industrial Park
China Post	November 2015	Guangzhou, Guangdong	Signed strategic cooperation agreement with Evergrande Real Estate
	May 2015	Jinzhou, Hubei	Best Express Jinzhou Distribution Center
	January 2017	Zhengzhou, Henan	China Post Zhengzhou Cross-Border E-commerce Industrial Park
Ane Express	August 2015		Signing ceremony for a strategic cooperation agreement between Ane Express and Yupei Group, a logistics real estate enterprise, to build an ecosystem of modern warehousing

TABLE 7.1

LOGISTICS REAL ESTATE PLANS OF EXPRESS COMPANIES

Meanwhile, the aforementioned Suning Appliance Group has also followed the trend, launching a series of high-profile projects in logistics real estate. On the evening of 13 November 2017, Suning.com made a public announcement stating that its wholly owned subsidiary Jiangsu Suning Logistics and Shenzhen Capital Real State had agreed to jointly establish a logistics real estate fund to invest in high-standard warehouses and logistics facilities, while seeking to acquire those facilities provided by other market players. With a final target of raising ¥30 billion and an initial target of ¥5 billion, the fund was to be invested in the warehouse project, which had a scale of 12 to 15 million square metres. The company planned to sell up to 5.5 million shares of Alibaba, or 0.22% of Alibaba's total shares, after which it would hold 0.82% of the shares of Alibaba.

In comparison, JD Logistics was on a higher level in terms of its development of logistics real estate. By the end of 2016, JD Logistics had acquired land totalling 3.9 million square metres in 15 cities across the country for warehouse construction. Later, on 8 August 2017, JD Group bought two plots of land in Beijing Economic and Technological Development Area (Yizhuang) at a price of ¥3.85 billion. On 24 October of the same year, JD Group launched its real estate business. Not to be outmanoeuvred, Cainiao, a subsidiary of Alibaba, also built its own logistics real estate in China, which now meant there were eight such real estate bases in total.

8

CHAPTER

BEFRIENDING THE FAR AND ATTACKING THE NEAR

We hope to take an active part in both the Belt and Road Initiative and the Guangdong–Hong Kong–Macao Greater Bay Area construction. According to the Belt and Road Initiative, it is our next priority to 'go global' together with our customers. At present, SF has rapidly broadened its scope of international business, but it remains true that more than 90% of its income still comes from the domestic market. Our global strategy is to start from zero, which will really take some time. Of course, enterprises can also accelerate the development with the help of capital cooperation. But we hope to continue at a more stable and steady pace, rather than becoming too radical.

– Wang Wei

AN ATTEMPT AT INTERNATIONALIZATION

With the entrance of global corporations, many Chinese enterprises are facing competition not only from these foreign companies (which have abundant capital and incomparable technical advantages) but also from their domestic rivals.

When the once stable market in China had been relentlessly divided up by multinationals, in order to win room for survival, many Chinese companies were compelled to advance into the international market. Since the 1990s, Huawei, Gree Electric Appliances, Haier, TCL and some other Chinese enterprises have begun to seek access to the international market. Despite many difficulties and obstacles, they have successfully planted their feet in the new territories.

Since then, Alibaba, Tencent and many others have also embarked on processes of internationalization. For example, Alibaba has taken advantage of its e-commerce capabilities and Alipay, using them as two major strategies to expand its foreign markets in Japan, South Korea, Malaysia, India and Singapore.

Unlike Alibaba, Tencent has expanded its international market with QQ and WeChat, two instant messaging programs. In addition, Tencent has increased its investment in overseas e-commerce and has bought a US$1.4 billion stake in Flipkart, an Indian e-commerce company.

The above mentioned represent only a microcosm of how some Chinese companies have expanded into international markets. SF Express, as one of those companies, has notably aspired to become an internationalized 'FedEx of China' (see Chapter 3). Due to the necessity and urgency of internationalization, SF Express has accelerated its pace, taking cross-border e-commerce as its starting point.

In October 2013, SF Express set foot in the Thai express market and opened a special cross-border delivery line from China to Thailand. Subsequently, SF Express set up a branch in Thailand and a division in Bangkok, the capital city. Later, it also set up a branch in Vietnam.

Nowadays, SF Express has rolled out its logistics and distribution network across Southeast Asia, covering Singapore, Malaysia, Vietnam and Thailand. It has also provided two-way express services between Thailand and China, Japan, South Korea, Singapore, Malaysia and Vietnam, and guaranteed that such deliveries will be completed within three to four working days. Its official website has also added a Thailand site, using English instead of the local language.

There are two reasons why SF Express has been able to expand its market in Southeast Asia so quickly. First, there are geographical advantages. Second, the existence of the Association of Southeast Asian Nations (ASEAN) means there is a large potential market. Owing to these factors, SF Express has decisively expanded into Southeast Asian markets and has undoubtedly seized a commanding position, setting an example for itself in terms of expansion into other international markets.

OVERSEAS OPPORTUNITIES AND DOMESTIC COMPETITION

With the popularization of the mobile internet and the rapid rise of cross-border e-commerce in China, many Chinese express companies, including SF Express, have acquired a solid foundation on which to expand into the international market. Data show that up to 2014, China's express business ranked first in the world for four consecutive years, with an annual business volume exceeding 45% of the total volume of the rest of the world. Overall, China had contributed more than half of the world's express growth rate.

Even now, China's express business remains a huge and growing market. In terms of the growth rate of China's major express companies, there is no sign of fluctuation or slowing down. According to data released by the State Post Bureau of China, from January to November 2018, the business volume of the express service enterprises in China totalled almost 45.3 billion pieces, compared with 40.6 billion in 2017. The growth rate is quite obvious.

However, although the industry maintains rapid growth momentum, it is quite difficult not to ignore the increasingly fierce competition. On 31 May 2018, Jack Ma, founder of Alibaba, attended the Global Intelligent Logistics Summit and said: "We will invest hundreds of billions of yuan. If ¥100 billion is not enough, we could add several hundreds of billions yuan. We need to reduce social logistics costs, which account for 15% of China's GDP, to less than 5%."

In Ma's view, it is Alibaba's mission to reduce logistics costs. Additionally, there is potential business value in making such a move. Ma is not the only one who covets a piece of this huge cake. Liu Qiangdong, the founder of JD.com, is also actively planning and building an independent logistics system. On 18 October 2018, JD Logistics formally announced its entrance into the personal express business.

With both Alibaba and JD Logistics encroaching on the high-end express market, SF Express is bound to be involved in fierce competition. In Wang Wei's view, since the competition in the domestic market is very fierce, it is necessary to expand into the international market. In order to survive, SF Express must go global.

Compared with the rapid growth of China's domestic market, the potential growth of Chinese companies in the international express market is more promising According to data released by the State Post Bureau, from January to October 2018, the year-on-year growth of China's nationwide express business was 23.9%, with 27.1% for intercity business and 38.4% for business in international markets including Hong Kong, Macao and Taiwan.

In an interview with *China Business News*, Yang Daqing, a contract research fellow at the China Logistics Association, said that although competition in the express market in China was fierce, the mighty rise of the Chinese middle class was providing opportunities for the internationalization of Chinese express delivery.

Previous research findings show that SF Express was a pioneer in going global. It has been reported by *China Business News* that, as early as 2010, SF Express had already set up branches in more than ten countries, including Singapore, Korea, Malaysia and the United States. In December 2016, it was officially granted membership of the International Air Transport Association. In 2018, SF Express's air routes to Japan, the United States, India and Singapore were opened.[51]

There are two direct potential benefits of SF Express's going abroad. First, it could reduce the competitive pressure from the domestic market and, second, the company may benefit from the process of internationalization. In addition, SF Express has deeper reasons to go abroad. Internationalization could integrate DHL's supply chains in mainland China, Hong Kong and Macao (see Chapter 4), as well as enable SF Express to build Ezhou Airport in Hubei Province in Central China (see Chapter 3). Obviously, Wang has a clear strategy in mind to build a nationwide and global airline network with Ezhou Airport as the hub.

A COMBINATION OF 'LIGHT' AND 'HEAVY' ASSETS MODES

Although SF began its international adventure earlier than other Chinese express companies, it has followed a narrow path. In Yang Daqing's opinion, other than advantages on the demand side, China's private express delivery companies have not enjoyed obvious advantages in the process of internationalization.

Xu Yong, director of the China Logistics Association, admitted in an interview with *China Business News*:

> *At present, China's international express market is dominated by the world's three largest express delivery companies. From an international perspective, the low-end markets are dominated by the postal services of each country, while the high-end market is occupied by the world's three major express services. If Chinese express enterprises want to snatch a certain share from the international market, especially to shake the existing market, they need to pay a great price for the change. Yes, they should be prepared to spend a large amount of money.*

In terms of size and revenue, SF is still far behind DHL, FedEx and UPS, the three largest international express companies in the world.

According to *Fortune*'s list of the world's top 500 companies in 2018, DHL ranked 119th with a revenue of US$70.5 billion, UPS ranked 138th with US$65.9 billion and FedEx ranked 180th with US$60.3 billion. UPS and FedEx account for about 85% of the US express market. In Europe, DHL has a strong presence, with about 70% of its revenue coming from overseas. Moreover, these companies have maintained relatively high growth rates. Data show that in 2017, FedEx's freight tonnage kilometres reached 16.8 billion, with a year-on-year increase of 7.2%.

According to FedEx's fourth-quarter report for fiscal year 2018, the company's revenue was US$17.3 billion, with a year-on-year rise of 10%, and its operating profit was about US$1.5 billion. This set of data suffices to illustrate FedEx's fast acceleration in business. In mid-2017, FedEx ordered 12 Boeing 767F freighters and 12 Boeing 777F freighters.

According to SF's financial report in 2017, its annual revenue was ¥71.094 billion, with a year-on-year increase of 23.7%. Its net profit was ¥4.771 billion, with a year-on-year increase of 14.1% over the previous year. Thus, it could very easily be concluded that SF is only about a sixth of the size of the three aforementioned big global express companies in terms of business revenue. SF now exclusively owns 49 aircraft, but there is a significant gap between this number and FedEx's over 600 delivery aircraft.

In order to narrow the gap, SF has adopted a flexible strategy in going global. To expand into overseas markets, it has applied a combination of light and heavy assets in its business mode. This means that in different markets, SF will choose to either establish its own depots, with its own investment, or seek strategic partners. More specifically, in some nearby markets, such as Southeast Asia, it has mainly established its own branches and self-operated depots. However, in more distant markets, it has mainly cooperated with international giants and local express delivery services.[52]

In order to effectively promote its internationalization, SF has also resorted to joint ventures. On 26 May 2017, SF began cooperating with UPS (whose business covered 124 countries and regions around the world) by establishing Global Express Holdings Ltd, with each company holding a share of 50%.

FROM THE COUNTRYSIDE TO URBAN AREAS

In the process of going global, Huawei, Gree Electric Appliances and SF Express have all expanded into the international market with a strategy called 'surrounding the city from the countryside.' This view is supported by the above-mentioned Yang Daqing. In an interview with *China Business News*, Yang said:

> *From the perspective of the investment market, the ASEAN countries, South Asia, Russia and Africa are all high-growth international express markets. Meanwhile, they are also markets that the European, American and Japanese international express giants have not intensively explored.*

In Yang's view, underdeveloped areas, exemplified by the Indian market, are often the locations where Chinese enterprises like SF will employ their internationalization strategies. According to the India Brand Equity Foundation under the Indian Ministry of Commerce and Industry, the number of internet users in India is expected to grow from 475 million in 2017 to 830 million in 2021. This indicates that e-commerce will be an impetus to India's economic growth. The agency predicts that India's internet economy will be about US$250 billion by 2020. Its huge e-commerce market has undoubtedly led to the doubling and redoubling of the growth of India's mailing business.

Of course, SF would completely agree with this. In 2018, the company saw a relatively significant increase in the business brought by its China–India special airline. While helping Xiaomi Corporation to improve the efficiency of its logistics system, the special airline also successfully transported 8 tons of anti-myocardial infarction medicine from India to China via an international cold chain on 15 November 2018. This was the first time that SF provided its customers with solutions in the field of international medicine transportation.

Subsequently, it was reported by *China Business News* that "in 2019, SF will accelerate its internationalization process, and will continue to launch new airline routes which include those in the Middle East, Indonesia and Southeast Asia." Of course, on the road to going global, SF not only needs to compete directly with multinational express enterprises overseas but also needs to find a breakthrough in expanding its international market, so as to develop steadily and gain a foothold in the international market.

HITCHHIKING THE BELT AND ROAD INITIATIVE

On its journey toward internationalization, SF has taken advantage of the Belt and Road initiative to expand its market in countries along the Belt and Road. In the past three years, the company's international business has increased by more than 70%, with its market value soaring from ¥270 million to ¥1.1 billion in 2016 alone. Although it accounted for less than 2% of the company's total revenue, the year-on-year growth was more than 300%, making international business the company's fastest-growing sector. Now, the overseas sector has about 93,000 corporate customers.[53]

This coverage includes several countries along the Belt and Road. During the 2016 Double 11 Shopping Festival,

SF carried cross-border e-commerce parcels between China and many foreign regions, the top six of which were Russia, the European Union, Ukraine, the United States, Belarus and Brazil. Three of these are countries along the Belt and Road.[54] The reason why SF was able to achieve such a good performance is that the company had sowed and tilled for many years before the Belt and Road initiative was proposed, and it was now time for the company to enjoy its harvest.

THE MOMENT OF GOING GLOBAL

In recent years, more and more Chinese enterprises have initiated a going-global strategy and there has been a boom in cross-border e-commerce. In September and October 2013, the Chinese president, Xi Jinping, launched an initiative to build a 'New Silk Road Economic Belt' and a '21st-Century Maritime Silk Road.' These jointly became known as the Belt and Road initiative.

In this new era, in which China has decided to embrace the converging world with a more open attitude, huge business opportunities can be found. Many Chinese enterprises, including those in logistics and the express industry, have seized opportunities for internationalization.

In 2009, Wang Wei, who had always focused his attention on the express industry, sensed the commercial value of the international express business and began to systematically build an infrastructure for it. In the same year, the Double 11 Shopping Festival (launched by Alibaba) made its debut. One year later, SF had already set up its business branches in Singapore, sounding the trumpet of overseas expansion.

In the following years, SF made every effort to broaden its international market and it is now providing express services in 51 countries, including Australia, Cambodia, Canada, India, Indonesia, Japan, Malaysia, Mexico, Mongolia, Myanmar, Singapore, South Korea, Thailand, the United States and Vietnam. SF Express's business network covers Chinese communities in many countries. Such services mainly include international standard express, international economy express, international small-size LTL, bonded warehousing, overseas warehousing, transit delivery, and other import and export services of various types and time-definite standards.

Of course, the success of SF is indispensable from Wang's precise strategic judgement. Wang believes that the Belt and Road initiative is bound to accelerate the pace of Chinese enterprises' going-out strategy. After President Xi launched the Belt and Road initiative, Wang resolutely accelerated SF's internationalization by gradually expanding its international market. Its service extended to more than 200 countries and regions. Lin Zheying, the deputy chairman of SF Holding, thus told a reporter: "After SF goes public, its internationalization will definitely be a top priority."

In Lin's view, SF's adoption of its internationalization strategy was mainly due to its own needs. First, SF's customers need it to provide fast, good-quality international services. Second, the business opportunities brought by the Belt and Road initiative enable SF to have more choices and more stakes in the market. Lin explained:

> *In recent years, we can see the Belt and Road policies have had very clear effects on the businesses of SF. The Belt and Road initiative and national strategies provide a shortcut for us to open up the international market. Our projects to set up warehouses in Europe and branches in Southeast Asia were carried out smoothly. I believe that in addition to the company's own efforts, the success should be attributed to the prosperity and strength of the country, its strategic position in global politics, and the positive effects of new policies. With the help of our country's fundamental policies, private enterprises will indeed benefit.*

In the process of internationalization, SF also cooperates with the national postal administrations of other countries. Lin exemplified this practice by citing SF's cooperation with the Estonian Post. In September 2015, SF established a joint express company with Omniva (Estonia's national postal service) to transport goods purchased online by consumers from China to Estonia, Finland, Latvia, Lithuania, Russia and other countries in northeastern Europe.[55]

Undeniably, it was the Belt and Road initiative that provided SF with opportunities to cooperate with some sovereign countries. In this regard, Lin said: "It is because of SF's efforts and business negotiations that these countries would prefer to cooperate with SF, and more importantly, I think it is also because they see the support of a strong China."

Lin's opinion is derived from SF's experience of expanding its international market:

With so many logistical institutions sponsored by the government to support our development, I feel secure. With the Belt and Road initiative, China has taken into consideration some major difficulties faced by enterprises that are eager to go global. This makes us feel much more confident and secure in going out. The next step we will take is to improve the company's business capability, to make it compatible with the supportive policies of our nation.

EMERGING MARKETS ALONG THE BELT AND ROAD

Objectively speaking, even without the Belt and Road initiative, there would be no turning back for the internationalization of Chinese enterprises. To some extent, the initiative merely serves as a catalyst for the enterprises' decisions. The fact is that entrepreneurs of Chinese logistics companies, including Wang Wei, had been trying their best to capture any kind of opportunity in international markets even before the proposal of the initiative.

Lin Zheying said: "In fact, if there were no Belt and Road initiative, I believe that many locations would not be suitable for setting up logistics nodes. But now the initiative has given us new opportunities that we didn't expect to have."

In China, SF has a strong home-field advantage. However, in the international field, SF is a latecomer that has had to adjust its strategies to compete with the big four international logistics giants, FedEx, UPS, DHL and TNT. Lin thus stated: "Well nurtured by the Chinese market, the strengthened SF now has enough confidence to compete for market share with the four express giants.

However, it is not as simple as it seems, even though we have the financial resources and the ability to go global."

Lin believes that SF must adopt the combined strategy of "befriending the far while attacking the near" and "emphasizing heavy assets while not neglecting light assets" when it comes to competition with FedEx, UPS, DHL and TNT.

The combination of light and heavy assets is SF's key strategy. For a long time, SF has used the self-operative mode in China, especially in mainland China, and has allocated its resources correspondingly. Therefore, in addition to purchasing vehicles and aircraft, SF has been devoted to the construction of its own airline hub, which is the first specialized freight airport in the Asian delivery industry and the fourth in the world. Naturally, this is part of the company's heavy assets strategy. However, in the process of internationalization, the overseas market, culture and economy are quite different from those in China. Therefore, there exist many uncertainties. In this regard, SF has adopted various strategies. Specifically, SF has employed the regular chains mode in such regions as Southeast Asia and areas with a relatively strong Chinese cultural base. However, in regions such as Europe and America, SF has applied a cooperative mode, in which it mainly cooperates with local express enterprises or international giants.

Lin further explained: "In my understanding, we have adopted a market-for-market strategy in distant places. In other words, we help each other to build each other's market." According to Lin, in the future, SF may well adopt the strategy of in-depth cooperation at the capital level, to realize its internationalization goals and eventually achieve a market exchange with its foreign counterparts.

In the process of internationalization, SF has attached great importance to commercial values when providing logistics services for countries along the Belt and Road. Lin said:

> *We will keep a relatively clear mind in deciding whether there are reliable partners or not. Meanwhile, we should also judge which countries have relatively stable trade policies. We will not participate in speculations and will attach more importance to efficiency while exploring overseas markets. … I will try to highlight SF's competence while making strategic plans. For example, before SF achieves the capability to start scale operations with unmanned aerial vehicles, I will not plan to seek our market in island countries such as Indonesia. But if we had the capability, Indonesia would be my first choice. At that time I'll fully use our advantage to invest enough resources in Indonesia to solve the problems that the country finds unsolvable.*

In Lin's view, SF should expand the markets in countries along the Belt and Road, because logistics connectivity has undoubtedly become the main focus of these countries. As a logistics enterprise, SF will explore the potential values in this sector as much as possible. Lin said: "The growth in cross-border e-commerce markets gives us more opportunities, and we should not hesitate to seize them. I believe it will be a new growth point for SF. Our overseas business is booming, and I expect that our international business will continue to grow exponentially in the future."

APPENDIX

WANG WEI'S SPEECHES

SPEECH I

Since the beginning of 2012, some serious problems have arisen in the operation of the company, which are mainly manifested in two aspects.

First, slowdown of income growth. In June 2012, the year-on-year increase in the number of express deliveries was 24.2%, 19 percentage points lower than the same period last year (42.85%), and revenue increased 32.21%, 7 percentage points lower than the same period last year (39.29%). What is worthy of our attention is the fact that the whole industry has maintained a rapid growth rate in the same period of time. In the first half of 2012, the year-on-year growth in the number of express deliveries of the whole industry was 51%, and the revenue increased 39.7%. Comparatively speaking, in the first half of 2012, SF's growth rate was significantly lower than the industry level. Our income growth also slowed down and was lower than the industry growth, which meant that SF's market share declined (from 28.19% in June 2011 to 26.7% in June 2012) and the company faced a very serious situation.

Second, declining profitability. Since April 2010, the cost growth rate has begun to exceed the income growth rate. Also, the gap between the cost line and the income line became wider and wider. As of June 2012, the cost line was still above the income line. The increase to cost and expense was higher than that to income, which means that we have no effective measures to improve the efficiency of resources and to promote the rationality of various costs and expenses. Without effective measures, profitability will be our major concern.

Why do these problems arise? How should we deal with them? I will first make a few comments about the causes of the problems, then provide some possible solutions.

CONSERVATIVE AND RIGID MENTALITY

First, our people are ignoring the external situation. Over the past few years, the company's business has been growing at a high speed. Naturally, managers at different levels have been used to concentrating on internal work and working hard to build up internal strength. Yet they have ignored market changes and customer needs, holding the view that if internal management is good, they don't have to worry about business development. However, as the external situation changes, such inertial thinking patterns obviously become out of date, which is hindering the development of the company.

Second, we are not interested in gaining merit, just trying to avoid making mistakes. Is it because it is difficult to innovate? Or is it because our managers are not good at innovation? No! To be frank, we dare not innovate simply because we are afraid of making mistakes and shouldering responsibilities. Over time, our staff become accustomed to such a mentality, and innovation will merely become a slogan.

Third, there is a stifling office atmosphere. People at management level are incompetent in implementing the company's mission. Believing 'the less trouble the better,' they are unwilling to air their opinions. As a result, ordinary staff are holding a negative and passive attitude, and poor communication of information and buck-passing may arise between different departments. The situation is worsening, which has resulted in a stifling working atmosphere and internal friction.

Such a mentality has aggravated the current situation. What should we do? First of all, I want you to realize that the current business situation is not rosy, that we are losing our due market share. The management level must set up a market-oriented, customer-centred business concept, unlock the ideological shackles, and achieve a mentality transition from "I can do what headquarters lets me do" to "I can do whatever as long as it is not prohibited by headquarters and headquarters should help me do it." As a matter of fact, we encourage any innovation that does not violate the law, nor deviate from the basic strategy.

FAILURE TO ESTABLISH A MARKET-ORIENTED AND CUSTOMER-CENTRED SYSTEM

First, there is limited understanding of the market. This year, a large number of business sectors failed to realize their estimated revenue, and many of them attributed the failure to the poor economic situation. But my question is, "Why is the whole industry growing quite well?" The economic situation is not good, so fewer people use express delivery; or we cannot provide satisfactory services, so fewer people choose to use SF? Which is the real picture?

Second, there is indifference to the needs of customers. How many managers know who their most important customers are? Have you maintained face-to-face communication with them to understand their service needs? Have you examined whether 'SF Service' has substantially improved in recent years? Have you tried to be the only express service provider for your customers?

Third, we are doing superficial competitor research. We always only regard four international express giants or five domestic major companies as our competitors and summarize some simple dynamic information about these companies, which can hardly play a supporting role in business decision-making. The fact is that in different market stratifications, we face different competitors. Taking key customer development as an example, we find that some large domestic enterprises often choose small delivery companies and freight forwarding companies as their service providers. These small companies get the 'total package' business volume from their customers and then 'subcontract' some or even most of the business to us. In fact, these companies are providing 'solutions' to customers, offering high-end services, while SF has unfortunately just become a porter, offering low-end services. Who are our competitors for our target customers and target markets? What do you know about their quotations, operations, services and management? Why do customers choose them instead of us? These questions need to be deeply understood and analysed.

I think the solutions are as follows. First, we should establish a working mechanism to understand customers' needs and meet them in time. Our couriers are SF's eyes and ears as they can gain first-hand information about customers; meanwhile, management should listen to the voice of couriers, so that good ideas can be translated into new and better services.

Second, we should provide 'package solutions.' We should provide a one-stop service for key customers, change the customer structure and enrich our service types. As a result, the revenue from our key customers will become the main source of revenue, and we should never ignore their demands and push them to our competitors. What we learned from our visit to Yokogawa Electric Machinery in Singapore shocked and inspired many of our colleagues. It is feasible to drive production from fully customized demands. Customized service can be realized on a standardized platform. Moreover, providing customized service does not require super-high-quality employees; they just have to work hard on system integration, process design and corporate culture.

Third, we should test our quality management with the value realized for customers. Unlike what we used to do, we should no longer equate a quality index with a failure rate index and should instead focus on customers' needs and improve management quality.

FAILURE TO TRANSFORM FROM 'SF CAPABILITY' TO 'SF OPPORTUNITY'

First, our strong operational capacity has not been translated into market share. The company's operational advantages (time-limited control, industry leading, terminal distribution advantages derived from huge operating resources, etc.) are not integrated as solutions so as to meet customers' needs. For example, a large B2B customer chooses both FedEx and SF as its logistics suppliers because "SF has no time limit commitment and FedEx has it," yet later on the customer finds that SF could have provided a faster service than FedEx. I can cite one more example. On the one hand, we push hard from top to bottom, and still don't know who our target customers are. On the other hand, a large number of customers have various demands, but they are not sure what services are provided by SF and what can be offered by SF.

Second, we don't have an innovative service model based on our brand advantage. After years of accumulation, SF has established a reliable and competitive brand image among its customers. For example, we have a purchasing agent service called 'special and economic.' When customers choose this service, SF is not only a trustworthy transportation provider but also a trustworthy buyer for our customers, and SF's brand can guarantee product quality. Therefore, it is not difficult to imagine the great potential of brand value in the fast-moving consumer goods market.

Third, we haven't maintained the closest relations with customers through service innovation. At this stage, domestic customers' demand for service innovation is not unattainable at all. If we can make small improvements on the basis of existing capabilities, we can take the lead in customer satisfaction, improve customer loyalty and establish a 'flesh-and-blood' relationship with customers. For example, while researching the 'land allocation' services in the market, we can build an open service platform with strong competitiveness and integrate such capabilities as direct operation, warehousing services and system docking.

To break this passive situation, we need to take action in the following respects. First, we should clarify our strategies. We need to have clear answers to the following questions: Who are our customers? Who are our competitors? What are we good at? What market opportunities can we seize? What market share should be acquired and can be acquired? How should we acquire these opportunities and shares? If we don't have a clear vision of these strategic aspects, it may directly hinder people's courage in innovation.

Second, we need to solidify decision-making procedures. Our current working procedures regarding product design need to be changed urgently. Product design should either meet or lead customer needs and must be subject to rigorous business logic reasoning. For each product plan, at least three questions should be answered. Who is the target customer (to determine the market capacity and sales target)? Who is the competitor (to examine the competitive advantage and formulate a marketing strategy)? What about our competence (to design the operation mode and determine the break-even point)?

Third, we should adjust our organizational labour division. Adjustment of the division of functions and responsibilities would enable us to contact customers more efficiently and to face the market and serve customers more attentively. The establishment of a demand management mechanism would provide a convenient channel for innovative needs in operation. I call on you to further understand and make good use of these two points.

A MISCONCEPTION ON PROFIT

Profit can be gained by reducing expenditure. This is a common misconception among SF management personnel. When the profit margin is emphasized, most managers can only resort to cost control and investment control. This is a totally wrong viewpoint. It only considers the immediate interests and reduces investment in exchange for high profit margins, and it may result in the loss of sustainable development.

We need to realize that every functional department and every business unit of a company should be responsible for gaining profit, yet they may adopt different means. For example, operating units should have the correct profit concept. We should consider the relationship between input and output when making business decisions. Through in-depth study of regional market characteristics, we can grasp customer needs and constantly improve the effectiveness of input by leading innovation and development, so as to create profit. As for the functional departments, they should create their own standard of resource input, taking into account the relationship between quality and cost. While constantly improving resource efficiency through streamlining and optimizing working procedures, they should take such measures as upgrading tools, equipment and technology systems so as to create profit. To sum up, profit can be gained through a scale effect, resource efficiency, process efficiency and technical tools.

INSUFFICIENT INCENTIVES AND PRESSURE

We should reform our management mechanism and establish a performance-based mechanism.

To resolve the problem of insufficient incentives, we will thoroughly reform the current salary system next year and abolish fixed annual salaries regardless of the work done. The fixed salary and extra bonus should be separated. The former should be linked with the responsibility of the position and the length of service, while the latter should be linked with the targeted income and the approved profit margin.

To resolve the problem of insufficient pressure, we will set reasonable revenue goals next year. Previously, each business district created budgets by simply reducing the growth rate based on historical data, but now we will determine business goals based on the total market volume, market share and the company's development strategy for each district on a year-on-year basis, and make periodic reviews and evaluations. For areas with the worst operating results in the same region, the regional leader will make corrections within a time limit. Those areas that cannot improve their performance will be eliminated.

Today, we are faced with a very severe business situation in which 'risks' and 'opportunities' coexist. All kinds of pressure will only make SF Express burst out more energy. "Today's choice creates tomorrow's SF Express." Let us encourage each other in our endeavours.

Wang Wei

SPEECH II

The year 2014 has witnessed SF Express's most drastic reform since the company was founded more than 20 years ago. We have set up many new business divisions, explored some new businesses and experienced an explosive growth in our total business volume. Yet, in my opinion, almost half of these practices have been unsuccessful. The main reason for the failure is our inadequate preparation and planning, which can be seen in the following aspects.

First, a poor talent pool. When stepping into a new field, we must have various talents, but we don't.

Second, deviated new business implementation. We generally carry out new businesses with rigid uniformity, which presents a dilemma. On the one hand, the new business calls for numerous changes, which is very difficult for the old personnel. On the other hand, promoting new businesses with great effort will harm the quality of traditional business.

Generally speaking, we took a brand new look in 2014, but we are still a long way from true success. I believe, with the exploration of new businesses, in 2015, we will achieve stable progress because we have a clearer mind in adjusting and optimizing businesses.

THE 'EXPERIENCE' YOU TREASURED MIGHT BE YOUR 'BURDEN'

In the past year's business development and transformation, I have valued my colleagues' attitudes, opinions and self-improvement the most. We didn't recruit new employees but gave many opportunities to our own employees instead, by which we hoped that our people could seize the opportunities, quickly improve their ability and master some new technologies needed to make their careers better.

But in the process, I think many of our colleagues have carried too many burdens, which limited their development. To be more specific, our employees have formed a mindset of simply delivering goods and unconsciously applied this mindset in new business development. I used to tell many colleagues: "Don't regard previous experience as 'treasure,' because the 'experience' you value is likely to be a 'burden.'" When we step into a new area, we should have a new mentality. Blindly following past practices was one of the most important factors that limited our development in 2014.

The second thing I value greatly is the business culture of SF Express. SF Express values respect and inclusiveness. But in some new business areas, many colleagues show a sense of self-importance, which makes many outsiders, even our customers, uncomfortable. The first impression you give to others is ignorance and arrogance rather than confidence, which makes me surprised and confused. How can people trained by SF Express be like this? Many of our new businesses are still in the exploratory stage, so we should be very humble so as to learn from others and communicate candidly with our customers, rather than play the role of experts. Otherwise, they will have a bad impression of SF Express.

The third point I lay emphasis on is the management of new businesses. We had poor management of new businesses, which was understandable, because we needed to learn the features and operating patterns of the new businesses from scratch. But it is unacceptable to make mistakes at some very basic levels.

Thus, I always ask myself questions such as: Why did our team make these silly mistakes? Why did the whole group fail to see the signs of these problems in daily operation to prevent the mistakes from occurring? Remember, even small mistakes can cause big problems over time, which can make a company miss out on market opportunities and thus cause big losses.

CUSTOMER SATISFACTION INDEX THIS YEAR? I DON'T BUY IT

The more business we have, the more attention we should pay to service quality. We have been insisting on hearing the real voice of customers from different channels. But as things stand, the means through which we get customers' opinions are questionable and, consequently, the authenticity of the data presented is questionable too.

The data, either monthly or annual, is very impressive, but to be honest, I can't really feel the improvement of our service quality. On the contrary, I think it is declining.

This was a terrible blow to me. SF Express has always taken integrity as the basic industry standard for employees. Why is there still cheating on some internal reports and data? This is totally unacceptable. It is under such circumstances that I think it is questionable that our customer satisfaction has increased this year. You may believe the data or not, but I don't buy it.

What goes wrong must be fixed, but how? First of all, the information we get from customers must be timely, authentic and accurate. Otherwise, we will not know the real needs of our customers or the problems they actually face. Consequently, there will be no way to improve the service. In addition, if we have no knowledge about our customers, how can we launch new products and new services with higher quality or added value, in such a way as to affect the achievement of the strategic goal of the company?

People like flattering data. But if they are not real and cannot reflect reality, what's the point of having them? The last thing we need is self-deception. A good reputation is derived from good service. SF Express did not have a marketing team in the first 18 or 19 years, and we promoted our business relying on word of mouth, which was the most effective marketing tool. Today, we have had our professional marketing team for more than three years. Do we still need to do marketing by reputation? All of us need to think about this. The brand value of SF Express must be supported by high service quality.

SF EXPRESS SHOULD NOT BE A COMPANY OF MANUAL LABOURERS

Someone asked me, what is the biggest problem I have encountered in the process of company transformation? For me, it is neither the management of more than 300,000 employees nor the strategic direction in the transformation process, but how to reduce the workload of front-line employees while ensuring their income or even improving their income when the company's profits are thin.

The express industry is a very tough industry. Couriers on the front line are intensively hard-working. If we can't get rid of the traditional labour-intensive model, SF Express will never transform successfully. My biggest regret in 2014 was not being able to come up with some effective solutions in this regard. It is hoped that in 2015, not only will we have a plan but we will also start pilots to implement it. I really don't have the heart to see my colleagues work in such a harsh and tough way.

Why have we tried so many new value-added services since 2014? Some colleagues may not truly understand this practice. Actually, we are looking for new business models to create more benefits, by which we could reduce both the working hours and labour intensity of front-line employees. It is not intended to hassle our staff. I have always believed that it is not SF Express's destiny to resort to physical labour in delivering goods. Our next target is to shift our focus from muscle work to brain work, from building SF's brand image to the creation of the personal image of employees.

The shift is a must. If each of our colleagues can change their thinking pattern and play an active part in the implementation of the company's strategy, our success will be around the corner. By then, all of us will benefit, and SF Express will make great progress.

A SERVICE-ORIENTED ENTERPRISE WITH INTERNET THINKING

SF Express is determined to transition from a logistics enterprise to a service-oriented enterprise with internet thinking.

Now we live in the era of the internet. Some people say that if traditional logistics enterprises like SF Express want to keep up with the pace of the times, it is necessary to recruit people with internet thinking. Yet I don't think simply bringing in such people can solve our current problems. More importantly, all of us should have internet thinking.

I think that the so-called internet thinking in the express industry means that we should respond more quickly, flatten the organization and try all means to meet customers' needs. This will bring great impact and challenge to traditional enterprises.

In the past, we provided highly standardized products and services. In order to respond quickly and provide more customized services, we must change our management and operation mode. This is the challenge we face.

Take Cantonese morning tea as an example – is it standardized or personalized? Both make sense. You go to a restaurant, open the menu and see hundreds of kinds of *dim sum* and snacks for you to choose from. You order what you like and all you need to do is to wait for three to five minutes, after which the *dim sum* will be served to you. This is a very personalized process. However, there is a fairly standardized process when making the *dim sum* in the kitchen. Everyone there has their own work, and food materials, ingredients and cooking time are specified. There is a scientific and standardized system in the kitchen.

Let me show you how the internet is applied in the industry nowadays. Before arriving at the restaurant, the customer has ordered via an app on their phone so that the chef can prepare in advance and the dishes can be served shortly after the customer arrives. This is a seamless process. The highly flattened supply chain will reduce costs and improve efficiency to the greatest extent and will improve customers' satisfaction in terms of price, service and personalized products.

What I have talked about above is part of internet thinking. One must see the whole industrial chain instead of one link, focus on upstream and downstream products instead of an individual product, and observe customers' needs instead of only your own business. At the same time, personalized products or services should be provided for customers to choose from. SF Express aims to transition from a logistics enterprise to a service-oriented enterprise with internet thinking.

What role will we play in the future? A hotel, a hotel's logistics provider, a hotel's information system or simply a consultant? I would say all. The key is to strike a balance so that we can meet customers' demands by providing suitable products. Meanwhile, the quantity and the customization of standard products will be adjusted in a dynamic way accordingly.

Take crispy durian pastry, a Cantonese dessert, as an example. Many people do not like its special smell. Hence, the sales volume is limited because only a limited number of people will come to order it in a local restaurant. But now, with express logistics and the internet sales model, this same restaurant may cover customers from the whole city. There may be only a dozen people who like crispy durian pastry in a community, but thousands of people may like it in the whole city. Naturally, the sales will be higher.

Today, internet thinking, just like sunshine and dew, has become an organic part of public life. Most of us are enjoying all kinds of services and conveniences brought by the internet every day. What kind of internet services do customers need? As long as we put ourselves in our customers' shoes, we will find the answer.

EMPLOYEES FIRST, COMPANY SECOND

No one knows what changes will take place in the market, let alone the policies and economic environment in the future. SF Express will actively try new models when facing these changes and will constantly make adjustments. But no matter how it may change, one thing will never change: that is, the company will always treat all employees with integrity, genuineness and sincerity.

Everything we do, including restructuring internal departments, gives priority to our employees. Of course, there are conditions for the employees too. The premise is that employees are sincere about the company, supportive of the development of the company and ready to embrace change. Consequently, our employees will not worry about being marginalized during changes and adjustments; instead, they will get more opportunities. We will resolutely crack down on those who are dishonest and unwilling to contribute, as well as those who seek illegitimate interests.

Everything we designed in the process of transformation has taken both the interests of employees and the development of SF Express into consideration. I will never prioritize the company's interests over those of the employees. As long as I am in SF Express, I will carry out the company's strategic plans and daily management with such an attitude.

In 2015, we will continue to optimize the reform we carried out in 2014. It is impossible to change strategic planning on a yearly basis. We will maintain the current plan for three to five years. We need to further develop many capabilities, including those of the supply chain, standard transportation, refrigerated transportation and the B2C [business-to-consumer] market service. As far as I am concerned, 2014 is a starting point, after which problems will occur inevitably. It is normal to have problems. The key is to find ways to solve them in time. Next, we will optimize and strengthen our business units, reduce our losses, improve our service quality, expand our scale and highlight our advantages in some new industries.

Wang Wei

SPEECH III

I have talked a lot about innovation, change and service previously. Today I want to talk about the supporting soft powers – namely, our belief, culture and morality.

BELIEF MAKES PEOPLE SELF-DISCIPLINED AND GRATEFUL

Many of my colleagues know that I believe in Buddhism. Why did I choose this belief? What has it brought to me? After my explanation, I believe you will have a better understanding of what Wang Wei and SF have done, and the future development of SF.

First, I set up SF at the age of 22. At the age of 25, the company started to take shape, and I earned my first barrel of gold. Some people said, "Wang Wei is talented, young and ambitious, but he doesn't have the brain to become a 'local tycoon.'" Frankly speaking, I was a typical upstart when I was 25 years old.

Let me share with you the background and reasons behind this story. When my family moved to Hong Kong from the Chinese mainland in 1976, we were quite poor and had to start from scratch. My parents used to be university professors, but their diplomas were not recognized in Hong Kong, so they had to work as manual labourers to earn low wages.

So we were poor, and knew quite well what it was like to be penniless and discriminated against. Later, when I was 25 years old and earned the first barrel of gold in my life, I felt a bit superior. I wanted to tell the whole world that "I am no longer what I used to be. I am a rich man!" I became a typical upstart.

Fortunately, this did not last long, for three main reasons.

First, as one's career continues to rise to a new level, one's vision and mind become different.

Second, I must thank my wife for pouring cold water on me to keep me awake and calm when I am too complacent.

Third, I found spiritual support and was converted to Buddhism.

In life, you can't control 99% of things, leaving only 1% under your control, and that 1% is your attitude of doing things. Your attitude contains two different choices. It is up to you to decide whether to adopt a positive attitude or a negative one – whether to accept mindfulness or evil ideas. If you make the right choice in this respect, you will magnify this 1% 100 times to make up for many other deficiencies.

Why do I want to talk about this? Because in the process of enterprise development, I gradually realized that my so-called success today is actually something accumulated in my previous life. In this process, the so-called ability is not the key point, but just a lucky reward stemming from the time, the place and the people gathered together.

Frankly speaking, I don't believe in coincidence. Why is there coincidence? Because ignorant people tend to believe in something accidental. When they suddenly win a prize, they do not know the reason behind it and just attribute it to a coincidence. However, if all the causes and effects are brought together, you will compare, and you will know that everything that happens is inevitable. What we need to do now is to use SF as a good platform to turn many seemingly accidental things into certainties in the future.

CULTIVATING COMPANY CULTURE TO ATTRACT TALENT

There are many Dharma stories in Buddhism. The purpose of these stories is to help people in the world "know rightly, become mindful and practice rightly." Although these are metaphysical principles, they can give people *samyak-smrti*, or mindfulness, a positive outlook on life and values. At the same time, they can be spread through the words and deeds of the recipients. These are more meritorious than giving people money and food directly, and a good corporate culture should also have such functions.

Every year, many people may get recruited by SF Express; meanwhile, we also have some staff who choose to leave. Why do some employees enter the company with great expectations and then walk away after a while? The reason is simple. Either they are treated unfairly or they are unable to get their needs met (both material demands and career development). But there may be a problem: it is not because the company cannot offer those leaving employees the things they need; rather, it is simply that we are not clear about their needs.

It's terrible. We can only transmit the corporate culture to current employees. But the problem is that people cannot fully understand our culture in the two or three months before they leave. Soon we need to repeat what we have been saying to new employees. It's like raising a child. When he's two or three years old, you tell him to love his parents and study hard. He just doesn't understand your point and knows only to reach out for food. Then when he reaches the age of puberty, he learns to rebel.

People grow up in this way, and it's the same for employees in a company. First of all, you have to recruit and get them on board. Then let them really integrate into the whole team, find a sense of belonging, and get a sense of honour by inculcating corporate culture, providing training and offering incentives.

Every one of us has been young, and please recall your mentality when you were young: What were we thinking about at that time? What did we want to do? What did we hate most? Naturally, we should learn to put ourselves in others' shoes and have an equal dialogue with young people in ways that are acceptable to them. We should never talk in a condescending tone and criticize them harshly.

We understand that different people may have different needs. Those who have some material gains and those aiming at survival may have different pursuits, and their daily needs and focus will also be quite different. How should we treat senior managers, new employees who have just been on board for one year and those who have served the company for more than ten years, respectively? We should take the following factors into consideration: age group, gender, years of serving the company and job-related rankings. Instead of attending to big and small matters all at once, we should pay attention to details and finish our tasks more systematically.

THE ISSUE OF MORALITY

Today's society has witnessed great economic development, yet people are becoming more impetuous. Many people are consciously or unconsciously pursuing *wei* (short for *weishui* in Cantonese, which means showing off and being arrogant). But few people clearly know the precondition for *wei*. Some people think that as long as people have money and authority, they can be *wei*. But that is totally wrong. It is not based on money or power, but on virtue. One walks in the street with one's head held high and people show respect and friendship rather than envy and hate. That is the essence of *wei*.

Here I want to tell all our colleagues in SF that we should understand its connotation correctly. Many people like to show off their wealth and power. This seems to me to be quite ignorant. They misunderstand the meaning of wealth and power.

In recent years, newspapers and media have been discussing that our people are discriminated against when they go abroad because foreigners are jealous of our wealth. What I want to say is that possibly they are jealous of us, but more importantly, they are not accustomed to our ignorance and improper behaviours. It is quite sad that a person's wealth is not proportional to their character and accomplishments.

If we want to be respected when we go abroad, we must first have moral integrity and learn to respect others. How to respect others? First of all, you should respect their rules and regulations. No spitting nor littering. Second, you should respect people's living habits. Be quiet in public places. Queue up while shopping or waiting for a bus. Finally, you should show respect to people's culture, different religious beliefs, different systems and regulations. Avoid provoking or offending others in everyday activities.

If you don't care about these details and 'do whatever you want to do' in a foreign country, you are doomed to be despised. Now SF has more and more overseas outlets, and more and more employees are travelling abroad. I hope you don't have such bad habits.

I also have my own standard to show respect – that is, to make the people who serve you happy. When I go to a restaurant for dinner, I will take the initiative to greet everyone I meet, no matter whether they are the manager or the waiters. The waiter also enjoys serving me because I am polite when talking with him. I want to make the waiter happy because of the message I have conveyed, which is called 'respect.' In contrast, some people are arrogant when they enter a restaurant. They shout at the waiter and have a very bad attitude. It is very difficult for such people to gain real respect from others.

Wang Wei

AFTERWORD

Two roads diverged in a yellow wood,
And sorry I could not travel both
...
Somewhere ages and ages hence:
Two roads diverged in a wood, and I –
I took the one less travelled by,
And that has made all the difference.

These lines are quoted from "The Road Not Taken," written by Robert Frost, an American poet. Some readers may think that it is not appropriate to cite these lines when telling Wang Wei's story, but I take a different view.

Wang was born into a well-off family and had an enviable childhood. When he moved to Hong Kong with his parents, he intended to work hard and be enrolled in the University of Oxford or the University of Cambridge, thus becoming the world-famous scientist he dreamed of being. However, fate played a big joke on him. Because his parents' diplomas were not recognized in Hong Kong, his family led a hard life.

Thus, Wang knew quite well what it was like to be penniless and discriminated against when he was young.

After graduating from high school, instead of studying at a university, he resolutely entered the workplace.

Like most children from grass-roots families, Wang became an apprentice, working in his uncle's factory. Later, the tide of going north and investing there gave Wang hope. It was at this moment that Wang started his small business. At first, he, like other Hong Kong businesspeople, invested in the printing and dyeing business, but unlike them, he saw potential for the express market. Thus, Wang "took the one less travelled by, and that has made all the difference."

The thing was, with so many people immigrating to Hong Kong, only a few of them became successful. Why did this happen to Wang? One of the key reasons was that he saw the business opportunity and seized it immediately. In 1993, Wang founded SF Express in Shunde, which began the history of SF Express. After Wang established the headquarters in Shenzhen, the company experienced leapfrog development. Wang told *Nanfang Daily* about the choice of this location:

> *I actually didn't think too much at that time and only came up with the following reasons. First, Shenzhen is close to Hong Kong. It is convenient for people and goods to go through customs, and it is also convenient for me to go back home. Second, compared with other cities, Shenzhen is more vibrant. In the late 1990s, it was an immigrant city. People there were quite energetic. Third, there is no 'burden' in Shenzhen. When young people come to this brand new land, their priority is to work hard and start their own career.*

In Wang's view, entrepreneurs need both innovation and courage. Therefore, under his leadership, SF Express has experienced several reforms, shifting its business mode from franchising to direct operating, which was the prelude of SF Express's reform. Later, Wang introduced a full-channel ecological environment, invested in logistics real estate and launched the strategy of going global.

However, SF Express, insisting on the heavy assets mode, began to be overtaken by its rivals due to fierce competition. At that time, Wang had to resort to the power of capital to meet these challenges by going public through back-door listing. At the same time, Wang launched a series of reforms to keep SF Express a leading power in the delivery business.

Under Wang's leadership, SF Express has made progress each year. On the evening of 26 February 2019, SF Holding released its 2018 performance report, which showed that the company's total revenue in 2018 was ¥90.9 billion, an increase of 27.6% over the same period in 2017. The net profit to be paid to its shareholders was ¥4.6 billion, 4.57% less than that in the same period in the previous year.

ACKNOWLEDGEMENTS

I would like to express my deepest appreciation to the excellent staff working for the Fortune Business School Book Series, who participated in the preliminary planning, market analysis, data collection, manuscript proofreading, text revision and chart-making for this book.

I would also like to extend my gratitude to the following people for their contributions to this book: Zhou Meimei, Wu Xufang, Jian Zaifei, Zhou Zhiqin, Wu Jianglong, Wu Chaonan, Zhao Lirong, Zhou Bin, Zhou Fengqin, Zhou Lingling, Jin Yi, Wang Yang, Lan Shihui, Xu Shiming, Zhou Yuncheng, Zhou Tiangang, Ding Qiwei, Wu Yufeng, Zhang Zhushu, Jiang Jianping, Zhang Dade, Zhou Fengqin, He Qing, Li Jiayan, Chen Desheng, Ding Yunyun, Xu Si, Li Aili, Li Yan, Huang Kunshan, Li Wenqiang, Chen Fang, Zhao Xiaotang, Xiong Na, Gou Bin, She Wei, Ouyang Chunmei, Wen Shuxia, Zhan Xiaohong, Shi Xia, Chen Desheng, Yang Danping, Shen Juan, Liu Bingquan, Wu Yulai, Wang Jian, Pang Zhidong, Yao Xinyu, Zhou Jingjing, Cai Yue, Jiang Lingling, Huo Hongjian, Zhao Lijun, Wang Yan, Li Rong, Li Wenqiang, Ding Wen, Li Aijun, Ye Jianguo and others.

One can never write a book without learning from previous research. In the process of writing, I have referred to relevant information in TV sources, books, the internet, videos, newspapers, magazines and others and would like to express my heartfelt thanks to the authors of the relevant literature. Please excuse me for any careless omissions.

Many professors, experts in business management, people working in media and marketing, and editors of the publishing house have given their unparalleled support. I gratefully acknowledge their help.

Last but not least, I wish to give my special thanks to my legal adviser, Ding Yingqiao from Dajian Law Firm.

Due to my limited time and knowledge, some mistakes and errors in this book are unavoidable, and I would like to welcome readers to offer kind criticism and correction via my e-mail: zhouyusi@sina.com.

Zhou Xibing

18 March 2019, Caifu Shufang

BIBLIOGRAPHY

Baidu Library. "SF Express Logistics Service Operation Analysis." Last modified 19 January 2016, https://wenku.baidu.com/view/dd2880f4376baf1ffd4fadb5.html.

Chen, Jiahe. "Leadership and Modeling: Unveiling the Veil of Competitive Advantage of Enterprises." *Securities Times*, 16 February 2019.

Chen, Shanshan. "Private Express Transition: SF Spends Hundreds of Millions on Scientific Research Every Year." *First Financial Daily*, 20 October 2017.

Chen, Shiai. "SF Expansion Sequelae: Market Value Wiped Out 163 Billion, Payable Bonds Increased Nearly 10 Times." Last modified 25 December 2018, http://finance.sina.com.cn/stock/s/2018-12-25/doc-ihmutuee2601354.shtml.

Christensen, Clayton. *The Innovator's Dilemma: When New Technologies Cause Great Firms to Fail*, Harvard Business Review Press; 1st edition (May 1, 1997).

Cui, Ningning. "Ruan Yuanyuan, a Hong Kong Man with 94 iPhones Was Seized by Shenzhen Customs." *Guangzhou Daily*, 13 January 2015.

Dai, Xiaoxiao, Hu Liangguang and Lu Li. "Dialogue with Wang Wei: SF Technology is the 'Boss' of SF Express." *Nanfang Daily*, 27 May 2018.

DHL, Deutsche Post Dhl Group and S.F. Holding in Rmb 5.5 Billion Landmark Supply Chain Deal, last modified 26 October 2018, https://www.dhl.com/global-en/home/press/press-archive/2018/dpdhl-group-and-sf-holding-in-rmb-5-5-billion-landmark-supply-chain-deal.html.

Dong, Jie. "SF's 'Protracted Retail War': Why Are They Repeatedly Defeated?" Last modified 14 June 2018, https://tech.sina.com.cn/i/2018-06-14/doc-ihcwpcmq8347321.shtml.

Du, Liang. *Drawing Sword*. Beijing: PLA Literature and Art Press, 2006.

Gold Rush. "How SF Helps Itself." Last modified 9 October 2018, https://www.sohu.com/a/258337958_100183344.

Foshan Shunde District People's Government Network. "Basic Survey of Shunde." Last modified 2019, http://www.shunde.gov.cn/zjsd/jbgk/1.

Huang, Zhan. "At the Foot of the Lion Rock." Last modified 2019, https://baike.baidu.com/item/狮子山下/6241560?fr=aladdin.

"The 'International Style' of SF Express the Maker: Launching SF Buy, a Cross-Border Ecological Circle is Taking Shape." *National Business Daily*, 16 March 2015.

Li, Hongxia. "Who Gave Shunfeng an Opportunity." *China Business* 3 (2017).

Li, Huaqing. "SF Holding Had a Revenue of Over 42.5 Billion Yuan in the First Half of 2018, with New Businesses Growing Rapidly." *Economic Observer*, 24 August 2018.

Luo, Min. "SF Intends to Issue Debt Financing Products Not Exceeding ¥16 Billion at Home and Abroad." *Shanghai Securities and Exchange*, 3 January 2019.

People's Network. "Brief Introduction to the Third Plenary Session of the Eleventh Central Committee of the Communist Party of China." Last modified 12 March 2019, http://cpc.people.com.cn/GB/64162/64168/64563/65371/4441896.html.

"The Reply of National Development and Reform Commission to the Feasibility Study Report on the Construction of the New Hubei Ezhou Civil Airport Project." Last modified 2018, http://www.ndrc.gov.cn/gzdt/201901/t20190116_925677.html.

SF Holding. "Annual Report of SF Holding Co, Ltd 2017."

SF Holding. "Notice on Renaming the Heavy Goods Group and Its Structure Adjustment."

Shao, Hao. "SF 43.3 Billion Backdoor Case Holographic Scanning: Equivalent to 1.25 Times of STO + YTO." *Shanghai Securities News*, 24 May 2016.

Sina. "Wang Wei is 70 Million Yuan Less than Ma Huateng: SF Holding Takes 400 Million Yuan as the Dividend for Shareholders." Last modified 28 February 2017, http://finance.sina.com.cn/stock/s/2017-02-28/doc-ifyavrsx5367625.shtml.

Sina Tech. "SF Best Changed its Head Again: Quan Guoshan as CEO." Last modified 26 September 2018, https://tech.sina.com.cn/i/2018-09-26/doc-ifxeuwwr8443031.shtml.

"State Post Bureau's Notice on the Results of Express Service Satisfaction Survey 2017." Last modified 30 January 2018, http://www.gov.cn/xinwen/2018-01/30/content_5262087.htm.

Tongdun Technology. "Company Profile." Last modified 2019, https://www.tongdun.cn/info/company.

Wang, Wei. "Innovation and Change: From 'SF Express' to 'SF Service.'" Zhongguancun 12 (2014).

Wang, Xiaowei. "SF Holdings Explains the Doubt of '30 Billion Liabilities': Related to the Direct Logistics Model, It Is Lower than the International Counterbid Giant." *Securities Times*, 18 January 2019.

Xiu, Boyu. "Sustainability of SF Retail E-Commerce Business." *Financial Economy* 2 (2019).

Xie, Dandan. "In the Express Industry with a Turnover Rate of 70%, Why Do Deliverymen of SF Express Work so Hard?" *Chinese and Foreign Management* 7 (2017).

Xu, Wen. "The Story of SF Express Going Out: 'The Belt and Road' is a Shortcut to Explore International Market." Last modified 18 May 2017, http://finance.sina.com.cn/chanjing/gsnews/2017-05-18/doc-ifyfkqiv6511101.shtml.

Yao, Yan. "Competing for the B-End Voice in the Logistics Industry, Shunfeng Throw 5.5 Billion DHL Integrated Supply Chain Business in China." Last modified 29 October 2018, http://www.sohu.com/a/271903216_419187.

Yu, Fangqian. "EMS and SF's PK." *Modern State-Owned Enterprise Research* 2 (2019).

Zhang, Cheng. "Express Pattern Fission: From Quantity to Quality." *Prosecution* 2 (2019).

Zhang, Huiqin. "Strategic Analysis of SF Express Against the Background of High-Speed Development of E-commerce." *Market Weekly* 2 (2019).

Zhao, Xiaoyan. "Tmall's Turnover Reaches 213.5 Billion on 2018 'Double 11' Day." *China News Agency*, 12 November 2018.

Zhao, Yue, and Tong Haihua. "SF's Overseas Journey: Significant Gap Between the Old Bidders and the Big Ones in Emerging Markets Has Huge Potential." *China Business News*, 30 December 2018.

ENDNOTES

1. The policy means: "We resolutely uphold whatever decisions are made by Chairman Mao. We unswervingly follow whatever instructions are given by Chairman Mao."
2. People's Network, "Brief Introduction to the Third Plenary Session of the Eleventh Central Committee of the Communist Party of China," last modified 12 March 2019, http://cpc.people.com.cn/GB/64162/64168/64563/65371/4441896.html.
3. Huang Zhan, "At the Foot of the Lion Rock," last modified 2019, https://baike.baidu.com/item/狮子山下/6241560?fr=aladdin.
4. The brand was founded in 1985. The founder of the brand, Nian Guangjiu, who is known as the 'King of Vendors' in China, is a self-employed man in Wuhu City, Anhui Province. He became rich by employing workers to process and sell roasted melon seeds.
5. Laoganma or 'The Old Godmother' is a brand of chilli sauce made in China. It was established in 1997 and is one of the most successful corporations to introduce foreigners to Chinese cuisine.
6. Li Hongxia, "Who Gave Shunfeng an Opportunity," *China Business* 3 (2017).
7. The 'Four Tigers of Guangdong' are Dongguan, Nanhai, Shunde and Zhongshan. They are four small and medium-sized cities with rapid economic development that rose in the Pearl River Delta of Guangdong in the 1980s.
8. Foshan Shunde District People's Government Network, "Basic Survey of Shunde," last modified 2019, http://www.shunde.gov.cn/zjsd/jbgk/1.
9. Ibid.
10. Ibid.
11. https://www.blueoceanstrategy.com/

12. Zhao Xiaoyan, "Tmall's Turnover Reaches 213.5 Billion on 2018 'Double 11' Day," *China News Agency*, 12 November 2018.
13. Xie Dandan, "In the Express Industry with a Turnover Rate of 70%, Why Do Deliverymen of SF Express Work so Hard?" *Chinese and Foreign Management* 7 (2017).
14. Ibid.
15. Ibid.
16. Ibid.
17. Ibid.
18. Ibid.
19. Ibid.
20. Ibid.
21. Ibid.
22. Dai Xiaoxiao, Hu Liangguang and Lu Li, "Dialogue with Wang Wei: SF Technology is the 'Boss' of SF Express," *Nanfang Daily*, 27 May 2018.
23. Luo Min, "SF Intends to Issue Debt Financing Products Not Exceeding ¥16 Billion at Home and Abroad," *Shanghai Securities and Exchange*, 3 January 2019.
24. Wang Xiaowei, "SF Holdings Explains the Doubt of '30 Billion Liabilities': Related to the Direct Logistics Model, It Is Lower than the International Counterbid Giant," *Securities Times*, 18 January 2019.
25. "The Reply of National Development and Reform Commission to the Feasibility Study Report on the Construction of the New Hubei Ezhou Civil Airport Project," last modified 2018, http://www.ndrc.gov.cn/gzdt/201901/t20190116_925677.html.
26. Wang Xiaowei, "SF Holdings Explains the Doubt of '30 Billion Liabilities': Related to the Direct Logistics Model, It Is Lower than the International Counterbid Giant," *Securities Times*, 18 January 2019.
27. Ibid.
28. DHL, Deutsche Post Dhl Group and S.F. Holding in Rmb 5.5 Billion Landmark Supply Chain Deal, last modified 26 October 2018, https://www.dhl.com/global-en/home/press/press-archive/2018/dpdhl-group-and-sf-holding-in-rmb-5-5-billion-landmark-supply-chain-deal.html.

29. "State Post Bureau's Notice on the Results of Express Service Satisfaction Survey 2017," last modified 30 January 2018, http://www.gov.cn/xinwen/2018-01/30/content_5262087.htm.

30. Ibid.

31. SF Holding, "Annual Report of SF Holding Co, Ltd 2017."

32. Clayton Christensen, *The Innovator's Dilemma: When New Technologies Cause Great Firms to Fail*, Harvard Business Review Press; 1st edition (May 1, 1997).

33. SF Holding. "Notice on Renaming the Heavy Goods Group and Its Structure Adjustment."

34. Du Liang, *Drawing Sword* (Beijing: PLA Literature and Art Press, 2006).

35. Li Huaqing, "SF Holding Had a Revenue of Over 42.5 Billion Yuan in the First Half of 2018, with New Businesses Growing Rapidly," *Economic Observer*, 24 August 2018.

36. Sina, "Wang Wei is 70 Million Yuan Less than Ma Huateng: SF Holding Takes 400 Million Yuan as the Dividend for Shareholders," last modified 28 February 2017, http://finance.sina.com.cn/stock/s/2017-02-28/doc-ifyavrsx5367625.shtml.

37. Dong Jie, "SF's 'Protracted Retail War': Why Are They Repeatedly Defeated?" last modified 14 June 2018, https://tech.sina.com.cn/i/2018-06-14/doc-ihcwpcmq8347321.shtml.

38. Ibid.

39. Ibid.

40. Ibid.

41. Chen Shiai, "SF Expansion Sequelae: Market Value Wiped Out 163 Billion, Payable Bonds Increased Nearly 10 Times," last modified 25 December 2018, http://finance.sina.com.cn/stock/s/2018-12-25/doc-ihmutuee2601354.shtml.

42. Dong Jie, "SF's 'Protracted Retail War': Why Are They Repeatedly Defeated?" last modified 14 June 2018, https://tech.sina.com.cn/i/2018-06-14/doc-ihcwpcmq8347321.shtml.

43. Chen Shiai, "SF Expansion Sequelae: Market Value Wiped Out 163 Billion, Payable Bonds Increased Nearly 10 Times," last modified 25 December 2018, http://finance.sina.com.cn/stock/s/2018-12-25/doc-ihmutuee2601354.shtml.

44. Sina Tech, "SF Best Changed its Head Again: Quan Guoshan as CEO," last modified 26 September 2018, https://tech.sina.com.cn/i/2018-09-26/doc-ifxeuwwr8443031.shtml.

45. "The 'International Style' of SF Express the Maker: Launching SF Buy, a Cross-Border Ecological Circle is Taking Shape," *National Business Daily*, 16 March 2015.

46. Wang Wei, "Innovation and Change: From 'SF Express' to 'SF Service,'" *Zhongguancun* 12 (2014).

47. Baidu Library, "SF Express Logistics Service Operation Analysis," last modified 19 January 2016, https://wenku.baidu.com/view/dd2880f4376baf1ffd4fadb5.html.

48. Gold Rush, "How SF Helps Itself," last modified 9 October 2018, https://www.sohu.com/a/258337958_100183344.

49. Tongdun Technology, "Company Profile," last modified 2019, https://www.tongdun.cn/info/company.

50. Gold Rush, "How SF Helps Itself," last modified 9 October 2018, https://www.sohu.com/a/258337958_100183344.

51. Zhao Yue and Tong Haihua, "SF's Overseas Journey: Significant Gap Between the Old Bidders and the Big Ones in Emerging Markets Has Huge Potential," *China Business News*, 30 December 2018.

52. Ibid.

53. Ibid.

54. Xu Wen, "The Story of SF Express Going Out: 'The Belt and Road' is a Shortcut to Explore International Market," last modified 18 May 2017, http://finance.sina.com.cn/chanjing/gsnews/2017-05-18/doc-ifyfkqiv6511101.shtml.

55. Ibid.

ABOUT THE AUTHOR

Zhou Xibing is a finance and economics writer, the founder of Caifu Shufang and the Zhou Xibing Platform, and a senior expert in localization management in China. He also works as a convener of Chinese family business issues and chief trainer for The President's Network.

With more than 20 years of experience in researching family businesses, he has profound, unique and systematic views on how to operate and manage a family business and how to carry forward family culture and business style. He has been praised by some media as a leader in family business research.

He has published more than 20 million words of financial works and some monographs on such enterprises as Apple, Chu's Orange, Gome, Gree, Huawei, Laoganma, Lenovo, Toyota and Wahaha.

He has been invited to give lectures and to write corporate case studies for dozens of CEO classes at some famous Chinese universities, including Tsinghua University, Peking University and Shanghai Jiaotong University, as well as some famous enterprises, such as Carpenter Tan, Chu's Orange, Gome, Gree Electric, Huawei, Laoganma, Lenovo, Tsingtao Brewery, Wahaha and XCMG Group.

His major works are: *You Can't Copy Laoganma*, *Huawei Methodology*, *Ren Zhengfei on Huawei's Internationalization*,

Ren Zhengfei on Huawei's Management Philosophy, *Ren Zhengfei on Huawei's Innovation Management*, *Starting from Heart: The Road of Carpenter Tan*, *How Traditional Enterprises Transform Themselves*, *How Chu Orange Became Popular*, *Why Gree Became No. 1 in the World*, *Learn Channel Marketing from Wahaha*, *Gree: Professional Management*, *How Family Business Achieves Long-Term Growth*, *Why Can't Chinese Family Businesses Be Passed On?* and *The Long-Lasting Successful Gene of Japanese Enterprises with a Hundred Years of History.*

Contact information for appointments about contributions, lecture invitations or strategic cooperations:
E-mail: 450180038@qq.com
Litchi Micro-lecture ID: Zhou Xibing Platform
WeChat: xibingzhou
WeChat official account: caifushufang001

CPSIA information can be obtained
at www.ICGtesting.com
Printed in the USA
JSHW020612071221
21036JS00001B/27

9 781912 555475